Oct 30, 1981
HAY FEVER

Cathy —
With Sincere th——
aND much Love —

THE
DRAMATIC
IMAGINATION

THE DRAMATIC IMAGINATION

REFLECTIONS AND SPECULATIONS

ON

THE ART OF THE THEATRE

ROBERT EDMOND JONES

Theatre Arts Books

NEW YORK

TO MY WIFE

Thirteenth Printing, 1980

ISBN 0-87830-035-X

Grateful acknowledgment is made
to the editors of the *Yale Review,
Theatre Arts,* and the *Encyclopaedia
Britannica* for permission to reprint
parts of this book.

Published by Theatre Arts Books
153 Waverly Place, New York, New York 10014

PRINTED IN THE UNITED STATES OF AMERICA

CONTENTS

INTRODUCTION

by JOHN MASON BROWN

THE THEATRE Bobby Jones believed in and created was a theatre that did not take the dim view and had not lost its sense of wonder. It was an extension of life, not a duplication, a heightening rather than a reproduction. The vision of what the theatre might be, as opposed to what it is, was present in almost every word Bobby ever wrote or spoke. On the printed page, as in his settings, he was our stage's high priest of evocation. No one who heard him could doubt his dedication, no one who saw his work question his genius. He was an unashamed pleader for beauty and, far more important, an unsurpassed creator of it.

"The artist should omit the details, the prose of nature, and give us only the spirit and the splendor," Bobby contends in *The Dramatic*

5

Imagination, and he practiced what he preached. "The spirit and the splendor," plus "an excitement, a high rare mood, and a conception of greatness," were with him life-long dreams which he turned into realities.

The theatre for him was always "an exceptional occasion." That is why Bobby hated it when its dialogue was dictaphonic, its concerns humdrum, or when it fed the eye on the drab, the non-selective, or the undistinguished. At one point in *The Dramatic Imagination* he says in a parenthesis, "It would be hard perhaps, to make the waterfront saloon setting of *Anna Christie* lustrous." Then he added, "But I am not so sure." In his case he had no reason to be unsure. Just as Midas had the touch of gold, Bobby had the quickening touch of radiance.

The ugliest scenes in real life throbbed with beauty when he had transformed them into scenery. Not as insipid or self-advertising prettiness. Not that at all. Instead they acquired a tension, a sense of mood, a luminosity, and a quality of drama which made spectators at once aware that reality had been lifted into theatre, and theatre into art. "Lustrous" was precisely what Bobby did make that waterfront saloon in 1921, even as "lustrous" to a greater extent is what he made the backroom and bar of Harry Hope's saloon in *The Iceman Cometh* twenty-five years later. Throughout his career this very attribute of being "lustrous" was an outstanding characteristic of his work, and one that set it apart.

I have to write about Bobby and his career in personal terms. Not to do so would be as false as referring to him as "Mr. Jones" and pretending that I had not known him long and fairly well. Since we were friends in spite of occasional disagreements, he was "Bobby" to me and his career is one that I followed almost from its beginning. As a matter of fact, the first article about the theatre I ever wrote for a newspaper was about him. It appeared in the *Louisville Courier-Journal* in the winter of 1919 under the title of "Craftsmanship of Robert Edmond Jones." I was then a freshman at Harvard who had been introduced the year before to a new world by "Mr. Jones's" unforgettable settings for *Redemption* and *The Jest*.

The first time I ever saw Robert Edmond Jones was when he came to speak at Harvard during my sophomore year. To those of us already stage-struck his coming was the cause of considerable excitement. "Art" with a capital "A" was very much in the theatrical air and this Jones man was known to us as one of its chief votaries and practitioners. We undergraduates who cared about the stage had not read our Kenneth Macgowan for nothing. We were steeped in Gordon Craig's *On the Art of the Theatre* and *The Theatre Advancing*, in Hiram Motherwell's *The Theatre of Today*, in Sheldon Cheney's *The New Movement in the Theatre* and *The Art Theatre*, and in the pages of Mrs. Isaacs' *Theatre Arts* (still a quarterly).

Bobby stepped onto the pink and white platform of the Music Building, wearing evening clothes as if they pained his spirit. His face was paler than the moon. He looked young, incredibly young. His hair was full and black, and in addition to the mustache he wore throughout his life he then sported a beard which, more than being "Left Bank," was almost sacrilegious.

He seemed shy, frightened really, and there was something about him of the holy man which he did not try to hide. It seemed to come naturally to him and we sophomores accepted him on his own terms. His speech, though hesitant, was sonorous. Most of what he said I do not now remember. I can, however, hear the richness of his voice. I also recall surrendering to his gift for conjuring visions with words.

Towards the lecture's end he confessed that he looked forward to the time (he seemed to see it right in front of him, too) when in the theatre the imagination would be set free, and realism abandoned because no longer necessary.

It was during that same season that Bobby did his celebrated settings for the Arthur Hopkins production of *Macbeth* in which Lionel Barrymore and Julia Arthur appeared. The revival, though a brave attempt, was a resounding failure. One reason was that the all too solid flesh and realistic performances of Mr. Barrymore and Miss Arthur were constantly at war with the symbolical abstractions of Bobby's scenery. On the Sunday before this *Macbeth* opened, however, Mr. Hopkins contributed an article to the *Times* which, tattered and yellowed is still pasted in my Temple edition of the play. I continue to cherish it as a statement of courageous intentions and particularly value the opening line which reads, "In our interpretation of *Macbeth* we are seeking to release the radium of Shakespeare from the vessel of tradition." When I came to know Bobby after my graduation and during my years on Mrs. Isaacs' *Theatre Arts Monthly,* I realized more and more that he was always trying to release the radium not of Shakespeare alone but of whatever he touched "from the vessel of tradition."

There are the cathedral and the Broadway approaches to the theatre. These are the two extremes. Bobby's approach, though he worked brilliantly on Broadway, was unquestionably the former. But it would be both unfair and untrue to suggest that he was a kind of grave St. Cecilia of scenic art. He loved life and he loved laughter, and his own laughter was the merriest of music. He was as ready to welcome the theatre of Valeska Suratt, Eva Tanguay, Olga Petrova, the Fratellinis, Bill Robinson, Florence Mills, or the Marx Brothers, as he was the theatre of Sarah Bernhardt, Duse, Chaliapin, Nijinsky, John Barrymore or the Lunts. His own desire was that what he saw on a stage, regardless of its level or kind, should be something different from life and more highly voltaged, something that had vitality and style, something that he could recognize and respond to at once as "theatre."

Jo Mielziner, who once was his assistant, says that Bobby was "the most practical of all dreamers." He assures me that, beautiful as his drawings were, Bobby never sketched for the sake of making beautiful drawings. The lines that he put down were always capable of realization on a stage. The Renaissance glories of his backgrounds for *The Jest;* the ominous outline of the Tower of London which dominated his *Richard III;* the great arch at the top of the long flight of steps in John Barrymore's *Hamlet;* the brooding austerity of his New England farmhouse in *Desire Under the Elms;* the background of mirrors, as bright as Congreve's wit, in *Love for Love;* the lovely Sunday-school innocence of his cutouts for *The Green Pastures;* the way in which he connected the portico of the Mannons' Greek revival home in *Mourning Becomes Electra* with the house of Agamemnon; the subtle suggestions of decadence in his living room for *The Green Bay Tree;* the bold bursts of Chinese red in *Lute Song;* or the George Bellows-like depth and shadows of his barroom for *The Iceman Cometh*—all these are stunning proofs of how completely Bobby was able to turn his dreams into realities and produce settings which lived as characters in the plays for which they were designed.

His driving hope was to give the theatre glory

and dignity and excitement. This he did again and again in visual terms and as no one else has done for our stage. If only more people at present dared to talk and write as Bobby did because they shared his determination and ability to restore dreams to our almost dreamless theatre!

THE REFLECTIONS and speculations which I have set down here are the fruit of twenty-five years of almost continuous work in the American theatre, during which I have had the good fortune to be associated with the foremost artists of my time. These thoughts have come to me in the midst of rehearsals and in dress-parades and on the long journeys to out-of-town tryouts and in the continual collaboration with playwrights and managers and actors and stagehands and costumers and electricians and wigmakers and shoemakers which has made up my life in the theatre. Out of the manifold contacts of my experience the image of a new theatre has gradually formed itself—a theatre not yet made with hands. I look forward to this ideal theatre and work toward it.

ROBERT EDMOND JONES

I

A NEW KIND OF DRAMA

*In art . . . there is a spark which defies fore-
knowledge . . . and all the masterpieces in the
world cannot make a precedent.*

—LYTTON STRACHEY

IN THE last quarter of a century we have begun
to be interested in the exploration of man's inner
life, in the unexpressed and hitherto inexpressible
depths of the self. Modern psychology has made
us all familiar with the idea of the Unconscious.
We have learned that beneath the surface of an
ordinary everyday normal casual conscious existence there lies a vast dynamic world of impulse
and dream, a hinterland of energy which has an
independent existence of its own and laws of its
own: laws which motivate all our thoughts and
our actions. This energy expresses itself to us in
our conscious life in a never-ending stream of
images, running incessantly through our minds
from the cradle to the grave, and perhaps beyond.
The concept of the Unconscious has profoundly

influenced the intellectual life of our day. It has already become a commonplace of our thinking, and it is beginning to find an expression in our art.

Writers like James Joyce, Gertrude Stein, Dos Passos, Sherwood Anderson—to name only a few —have ventured boldly into the realm of the subjective and have recorded the results of their exploration in all sorts of new and arresting forms. The stream-of-consciousness method of writing is an established convention of literature. It is readily accepted by the public and is intelligible to everyone. We find it easier today to read *Ulysses* than to read *Lord Ormont and His Aminta,* and we are no longer bewildered by *A Rose Is a Rose Is a Rose Is a Rose.*

Our playwrights, too, have begun to explore this land of dreams. They are casting about for ways in which to express the activity of the subconscious mind, to express thought before it becomes articulate. They are seeking to penetrate beneath the surface of our everyday life into the stream of images which has its source in the deep unknown springs of our being. They are attempting to express directly to the audience the unspoken thoughts of their characters, to show us not only the patterns of their conscious behavior but the pattern of their subconscious lives. These adventures into a new awareness of life indicate a trend in dramatic writing which is bound to become more clearly understood. But in their search for ways in which to embody this new awareness they have neglected to observe that there has recently come into existence the perfect medium for expressing the Unconscious in terms of the theatre. This medium is the talking picture.

In the simultaneous use of the living actor and the talking picture in the theatre there lies a wholly new theatrical art, whose possibilities are as infinite as those of speech itself.

There exists today a curious misconception as to the essential nature of motion pictures. We accept them unthinkingly as objective transcripts of life, whereas in reality they are subjective images of life. This fact becomes evident at once if we think of some well-known motion-picture star appearing in person on a stage and then of the same star appearing on the screen, a bodiless echo, a memory, a dream. Each self has its own reality, but the one is objective and the other is subjective. Motion pictures are our thoughts made visible and audible. They flow in a swift succession of images, precisely as our thoughts do, and their speed, with their flashbacks—like sudden up-rushes of memory—and their abrupt transitions from one subject to another, approximates very closely the speed of our thinking. They have the rhythm of the thought-stream and the same uncanny ability to move forward or backward in space or time, unhampered by the rationalizations of the conscious mind. They project pure thought, pure dream, pure inner life.

Here lies the potential importance of this new invention. A new medium of dramatic expression has become available at the very moment when it is most needed in the theatre. Our dramatists now have it in their power to enlarge the scope of their dramas to an almost infinite extent by the use of these moving and speaking images. Some new playwright will presently set a motion-picture screen on the stage above and behind his actors and will reveal simultaneously the two worlds of the Conscious and the Unconscious which together make up the world we live in—the outer world and the inner world, the objective world of actuality and the subjective world of motive. On the stage we shall see the actual characters of the drama; on the screen we shall see their hid-

den secret selves. The drama will express the behavior of the characters set against a moving background, the expression of their subconscious mind
—a continuous action and interaction.

All art moves inevitably toward this new syn-
thesis of actuality and dream. Our present forms
of drama and theatre are not adequate to express
our newly enlarged consciousness of life. But
within the next decade a new dimension may be
added to them, and the eternal subject of drama
—the conflict of Man and his Destiny—will take
on a new significance.

II

ART IN THE THEATRE

II

ART IN THE THEATRE

Art . . . teaches to convey a larger sense by simpler symbols.
—EMERSON

THERE seems to be a wide divergence of opinion today as to what the theatre really is. Some people say it is a temple, some say it is a brothel, some say it is a laboratory, or a workshop, or it may be an art, or a plaything, or a corporation. But whatever it is, one thing is true about it. There is not enough fine workmanship in it. There is too much incompetence in it. The theatre demands of its craftsmen that they know their jobs. The theatre is a school. We shall never have done with studying and learning. In the theatre, as in life, we try first of all to free ourselves, as far as we can, from our own limitations. Then we can begin to practice "this noble and magicall art." Then we may begin to dream.

When the curtain rises, it is the scenery that sets the key of the play. A stage setting is not a background; it is an environment. Players act in a setting, not against it. We say, in the audience, when we look at what the designer has made, before anyone on the stage has time to move or speak, "Aha, I see! It's going to be like *that!* Aha!" This is true no matter whether we are looking at a realistic representation of Eliza crossing the ice or at the setting for one of Yeats' *Plays for Dancers,* carried to the limit of abstract symbolism. When I go to the theatre, I want to get an eyeful. Why not? I do not want to have to look at one of the so-called "suggestive" settings, in which a single Gothic column is made to do duty for a cathedral; it makes me feel as if I had been invited to some important ceremony and had been given a poor seat behind a post. I do not want to see any more "skeleton stages" in which a few architectural elements are combined and re-combined for the various scenes of a play, for after the first half hour I invariably discover that I have lost the thread of the drama. In spite of myself, I have become fascinated, wondering whether the castle door I have seen in the first act is going to turn into a refectory table in the second act or a hope-chest in the last act. No, I don't like these clever, falsely economical contraptions. And I do not want to look at a setting that is merely smart or novel or *chic*, a setting that tells me that it is the latest fashion, as though its designer had taken a flying trip like a spring buyer and brought back a trunk full of the latest styles in scenery.

I want my imagination to be stimulated by what I see on the stage. But the moment I get a sense of ingenuity, a sense of effort, my imagination is not stimulated; it is starved. That play is finished as far as I am concerned. For I have come to the theatre to see a play, not to see the work done on a play.

A good scene should be, not a picture, but an image. Scene-designing is not what most people imagine it is—a branch of interior decorating. There is no more reason for a room on a stage to be a reproduction of an actual room than for an actor who plays the part of Napoleon to be Napoleon or for an actor who plays Death in the old morality play to be dead. Everything that is actual must undergo a strange metamorphosis, a kind of sea-change, before it can become truth in the theatre. There is a curious mystery in this. You will remember the quotation from *Hamlet:*

My father!—methinks I see my father.
O where, my lord?
In my mind's eye, Horatio.

Stage-designing should be addressed to this eye
of the mind. There is an outer eye that observes,
and there is an inner eye that sees. A setting
should not be a thing to look at in itself. It can,
of course, be made so powerful, so expressive, so
dramatic, that the actors have nothing to do after
the curtain rises but to embroider variations on
the theme the scene has already given away. The
designer must always be on his guard against being too explicit. A good scene, I repeat, is not a
picture. It is something seen, but it is something
conveyed as well: a feeling, an evocation. Plato
says somewhere, "It is beauty I seek, not beautiful
things." This is what I mean. A setting is not
just a beautiful thing, a collection of beautiful
things. It is a presence, a mood, a warm wind fan-
ning the drama to flame. It echoes, it enhances,
it animates. It is an expectancy, a foreboding, a
tension. It says nothing, but it gives everything.

Do not think for a moment that I am advising
the designer to do away with actual objects on
the stage. There is no such thing as a symbolic

chair. A chair is a chair. It is in the arrangement of the chairs that the magic lies. Molière, Gordon Craig said, knew how to place the chairs on his stage so they almost seemed to speak. In the balcony scene from *Romeo and Juliet* there must be a balcony, and there must be moonlight. But it is not so important that the moon be the kind of moon that shines down on Verona as that Juliet may say of it:

O, swear not by the moon, the inconstant moon . . .
Lest that thy love prove likewise variable.

The point is this: it is not the knowledge of the atmospheric conditions prevailing in northern Italy which counts, but the response to the lyric, soaring quality of Shakespeare's verse.

The designer creates an environment in which all noble emotions are possible. Then he retires. The actor enters. If the designer's work has been good, it disappears from our consciousness at that moment. We do not notice it any more. It has apparently ceased to exist. The actor has taken the stage; and the designer's only reward lies in the praise bestowed on the actor.

Well, now the curtain is up and the play has begun.

When I go to the theatre to see a play performed, I have got to be interested in the people
who are performing it. They must, as the saying
goes, "hold" me. It is my right as a member of
the audience to find men and women on the stage
who are alive. I want to respect these players, to
look up to them, to care for them, to love them.
I want them to speak well, to move well, to give
out energy and vitality and eagerness. I do not
wish to look at the physically unfit, the mentally
defective, or the spiritually violated. They bring
to my mind Barnum's cruel remark that normal
people are not worth exhibiting. I wish to see
actors in whom I can believe—thoroughbreds,
people who are "all there." Every play is a living
dream: your dream, my dream—and that dream
must not be blurred or darkened. The actors must
be transparent to it. They may not exhibit. Their
task is to reveal.

To reveal. To move in the pattern of a great
drama, to let its reality shine through. There is
no greater art than this. How few actors live up
to its possibilities! Some actors have even made
me feel at times that they were at heart a little
bit ashamed of being actors. I call this attitude
offensive. The right attitude is that of the dis-

tinguished old English character actor who, when engaged to play a part, was accustomed to say, "Sir, my fee is so-and-so much," as if he were a specialist from Harley Street. It is easy, of course, to understand why there are not more good actors on the stage today. The métier is too hard. This art of acting demands a peculiar humility, a concentration and dedication of all one's energies. But when an actor moves before us at last with the strange freedom and calm of one possessed by the real, we are stirred as only the theatre can stir us.

I am thinking of the company of Irish Players from the Abbey Theatre in Dublin who first gave us the dramas of Synge and Yeats in 1910. As one watched these players, one saw what they knew. I kept saying to myself on that first evening: Who are these rare beings? Where did they come from? How have they spent their lives? Who are their friends? What music they must have heard, what books they must have read, what emotions they must have felt! They literally enchanted me. They put me under a spell. And when the curtain came down at the end of the play, they had become necessary to me. I have often asked myself since that time how it was that actors could make me feel such strange emotions of trouble and wonder; and I find the answer now, curiously enough, in an address spoken by a modern Irish poet to the youth of Ireland— *Keep in your souls some images of magnificence.* These Irish players had kept in their souls some images of magnificence.

Exceptional people, distinguished people, superior people, people who can say, as the old Negro said, "I got a-plenty music in me." These are the actors the theatre needs.

I think it needs also actors who have in them a kind of wildness, an exuberance, a take-it-or-leave-it quality, a dangerous quality. We must get clean away from the winning, ingratiating, I-hope-you're-all-going-to-like-me-because-I-need-the-money quality of a great deal of the acting we find today. I remember Calvé's entrance in the first act of *Carmen.* Her audiences were actually afraid of her. Who has seen Chaliapin in the mad scene of *Boris?* Some of the best actors in the world are to be found on the operatic stage. What a Hedda Gabler Mary Garden would have made! It seems as if these actor-images were set free by the very limitations of opera—the fixed melodies, the measured steps and pauses. They cannot be casual for one instant. They must be aware. They must know how to do what they have to do. They must have style. And they must have voices.

It is surprisingly difficult to find actors who seem to mean what they say. How often one is tempted to call out to them from the audience, "It's a lie! I don't believe a word of it!" A deep sincerity, a voice that comes from the center of the self, is one of the rarest things to be found on the stage today. It seems odd that this quality of conviction should be so hard to find in the theatre.

But I have been speaking of actors, not of acting.

Great roles require great natures to interpret them. Half our pleasure in seeing a play lies in our knowledge that we are in the presence of artists. But this pleasure of watching the artists themselves is soon forgotten, if the play is well performed, in the contagious excitement of watching a miracle: the miracle of incarnation. For acting is a process of incarnation. Just that. And it is a miracle. I have no words to express what I feel about this subtle, ancient, sacred art— the marvel of it, the wonder, the meaning. The designer creates with inanimate materials: canvas, wood, cloth, light. The actor creates in his living self. And just as the good designer retires in favor of the actor, so does the good actor withdraw his personal self in favor of the character he is playing. He steps aside. The character lives in him. You are to play Hamlet, let us say—not narrate Hamlet, but *play* Hamlet. Then you become his host. You invite him into yourself. You lend him your body, your voice, your nerves; but it is Hamlet's voice that speaks, Hamlet's impulses that move you. We may be grateful to Pirandello for showing us, in his *Six Characters in Search of an Author,* the strange reality of the creations of the playwright's mind. Hamlet is as real as you or I. To watch a character develop from the first flashes of contact in the actor's mind to the final moment when the character steps on the stage in full possession of the actor, whose personal self looks on from somewhere in the background, is to be present at a great mystery. No wonder the ancient dramas were initiation-ceremonies; all acting is an initiation, if one can see it so, an initiation into what Emerson calls "the empire of the real." To spend a lifetime in practicing and perfecting this art of speaking with tongues other than one's own is to live as greatly as one can live.

But the curtain is up, and the play has begun.
We look into a scene that is filled with excitement. See. That man is playing the part of a beggar. We know he is not a real beggar. Why not?
How do we know? We cannot say. But we know
he is not a beggar. When we look at him we recall, not any particular beggar we may happen to
have seen that day, but all beggars we have ever
seen or read about. And all our ideas of misery
and helplessness and loneliness rush up in our imaginations to touch us and hurt us. The man is
acting.

How is he dressed? (And now I am speaking
as a costume-designer.) The man is in rags. Just
rags. But why do we look at him with such interest? If he wore ordinary rags we wouldn't look
at him twice. He is dressed, not like a real beggar,
but like a painting of a beggar. No, that's not
quite it. But as he stands there or moves about
we are continually reminded of great paintings—
paintings like those of Manet, for instance. There
is a curious importance about this figure. We shall
remember it. Why? We cannot tell. We are looking at something *theatrical*. These rags have been
arranged—"composed" the painters call it—by

the hand of an artist. We feel, rather than see, an indescribable difference. These rags have somehow ceased to be rags. They have been transformed into moving sculpture.

I am indebted to the great Madame Freisinger for teaching me the value of simplicity in the theatre. I learned from her not to torture materials into meaningless folds, but to preserve the long flowing line, the noble sweep. "Let us keep this production noble," she would say to me. The costume-designer should steer clear of fashionableness. That was the only fault of the admirable production of *Hamlet* in modern dress. It was so *chic* that it simpered. I remember that in the closet scene, as the Queen cried out:

O Hamlet, thou hast cleft my heart in twain.

and her son answered:

O, throw away the worser part of it,
And live the purer with the other half,

a voice near me whispered, "I wonder if she got that negligee at Bendel's?" And the program told us all that Queen Gertrude of Denmark did, indeed, get that negligee at Bendel's. And, furthermore, that Queen Gertrude's shoes came from the firm of I. Miller, Inc., and that her hats were furnished by Blank and her jewels by Dash, and so on. Think of it. Two worlds are meeting in this play, in this scene—in the night, in Elsinore. And we are reminded of shoes and frocks!

Many of the costumes I design are intentionally somewhat indefinite and abstract. A color, a shimmer, a richness, a sweep—and the actor's presence! I often think of a phrase I once found in an old drama that describes the first entrance of the heroine. It does not say, "She wore a taffety petticoat or a point lace-ruff or a farthingale"; it says, "She came in like starlight, hid in jewels." There she is in that phrase; not just a beautiful girl dressed up in a beautiful dress, but a presence —arresting, ready to act, enfolded in light. It isn't just light, it is a stillness, an awareness, a kind of breathlessness. We ought to look at the actors and say, Why! I never saw people like *that* before! I didn't know people looked like *that!*

The subtlety of stage lighting, the far-flung magic of it! When a single light-bulb wrongly placed may reveal, as Yeats said, the proud fragility of dreams!

Shakespeare knew more than all of us. How he uses sunlight, moonlight, candlelight, torchlight, starlight! Imagine Hamlet as he stands with Rosencrantz and Guildenstern on the forestage of the Globe Theatre, under the open sky, looking up at the stars, saying:

. . . this brave o'erhanging firmament,
this majestical roof fretted with golden fire. . . .

I have often wondered whether the Globe Theatre and the Swan Theatre were not oriented towards the east as ancient temples are, in order to take advantage of the lighting effects of nature. Think of the play of *Macbeth*. It begins on a foggy afternoon before sundown. The day goes. The sun sets. Torches are brought in. We enter deeper and deeper with the play into an extravagant and lurid night of the soul. Or take the trial scene from *The Merchant of Venice*. The scene is played by torchlight. The auditorium is dark. We see the sky overhead. The trial draws to an end. Shylock is defeated. There is a gay little interlude, the byplay with the rings. The stage grows lighter. The torches are carried off. Now the scene is finished. Portia, Nerissa, and Gratiano go away. . . . The full moon rises over the wall of the theatre and touches the stage with silver. Lorenzo and Jessica enter, hand in hand.

. . . on such a night
Did Thisbe fearfully o'ertrip the dew. . . .

The sole aim of the arts of scene-designing, costuming, lighting, is, as I have already said, to enhance the natural powers of the actor. It is for the director to call forth these powers and urge them into the pattern of the play.

The director must never make the mistake of imposing his own ideas upon the actors. Acting is not an imitation of what a director thinks about a character; it is a gradual, half-conscious unfolding and flowering of the self into a new personality. This process of growth should be sacred to the director. He must be humble before it. He must nourish it, stimulate it, foster it in a thousand ways. Once the actors have been engaged, he should address himself to their highest powers. There is nothing they cannot accomplish. In this mood, ignoring every limitation, he fuses them into a white energy. The director energizes; he animates. That is what Max Reinhardt understands so well how to do. He is an animator. A curious thing, the animating quality. Stanislavsky had it; Belasco had it; Arthur Hopkins has it. One feels it instantly when one meets these men. One sees in them what Melville calls "the strong, sustained and mystic aspect." The greatest stage director I ever heard of, incidentally, is Captain Ahab in Melville's *Moby Dick*. Turn to the scene of the crossed lances and read how Ahab incites the crew of the *Pequod* to hunt the white Whale to the death: *"It seemed as though by some nameless, interior volition, he would fain have shocked into them the same fiery emotion accumulated within the Leyden jar of his own magnetic life. . . ."* That is stage-directing, if you please.

Now I come to the playwrights. I am not one of the calamity-howlers who believe the theatre is in a dying condition. On the contrary. The American Theatre, as the advertisements of the revue, *Americana,* said, is a "star-spangled wow." And at all times we have before us the heartening example of Eugene O'Neill, whose work would be outstanding in any period of the world's dramatic history. But to my way of thinking, many of the playwrights of today are being swamped by their own facility, snowed under by their very cleverness. A kind of tacit conspiracy seems to be on foot to rob the theatre of its ancient mystery and its ancient awe. We seem somehow to have lost the original immediate experience of the theatre. Familiarity has bred contempt. In the dramas of today one feels an odd secondary quality. They are, so to speak, accessories after the fact. Our playwrights give us schemes for drama, recipes for drama, designs for drama, definitions of drama. They explain drama with an elaborate, beguiling ingenuity. But in so doing they explain it away. Instead of trying to raise us to the imaginative level of true dramatic creation, they have brought the theatre down to our own level. And so the ancient audacity has vanished, the danger, the divine caprice. The wonderful wild creature has been tamed. Our theatre has become harmless, and definite, and amiable. The splendid vision has faded into the light of common day.

There is nothing wrong with this recipe-theatre of ours except that it isn't the real thing. There is no dramatic nourishment in it. We are hungry, and we are given a cook-book to eat instead of a meal. We expect to go on a journey, and we have to be satisfied with a map and a time table. So long as this secondary art, this substitute theatre, continues to be their image of the theatre, our playwrights will continue to belong not with the artists but with the fabricators of the theatre.

And now I have come to my real point. I know that there are young people in this country who will really create for the theatre of their time, who will bring something into existence there that has never existed before. A few. Not many. The theatre will be fortunate if it can claim a half-dozen of them. But it is this half-dozen to whom we look to lift our common experience into a higher region, a clearer light. We do not want shrewdness or craftiness or adroitness from them. We have had enough mechanism in the theatre, and more than enough. Let them go beyond this; let them give us the sense of the dramatic moment, the immortal moment.

Think of this moment. All that has ever been is in this moment; all that will be is in this moment. Both are meeting in one living flame, in this unique instant of time. This is drama; this is theatre—*to be aware of the Now.*

But how is one to come aware? someone may ask. I answer, Listen to the poets. They can tell you.

Of all people in the world, Sir Philip Sidney

said, poets are the least liars. Poets are reporters.
They set down what they see. I will give you an
example from *Hamlet:*

> *O good Horatio . . .*
> *If thou didst ever hold me in thy heart*
> *Absent thee from felicity awhile. . . .*

Absent thee from felicity awhile. Here are some
of the most beautiful words ever written in the
English language. But this is not all. These words
are a plain record of fact. Hamlet, drawing his
last breath as he spoke them, was not interested
in phrasemaking, nor was Shakespeare. Hamlet
did not think up an exquisite phrase at that moment. He spoke out of a real vision of felicity,
immortal. He saw the clear light, the happy
forms. He saw the felicity. He called it felicity.

I could give you hundreds of examples. Poets
know that what they see is true. If it were not
so, they would have told you.

Nothing can stop progress in the American
theatre except the workers themselves. To them I
say: There are no limitations there except your
own limitations. Lift it. Get the personal *you* out
of your work. Who cares about *you?* Get the

wonder into it. Get your dreams into it. Where are your dreams?

Great drama does not deal with cautious people. Its heroes are tyrants, outcasts, wanderers. From Prometheus, the first of them all, the thief who stole the divine fire from heaven, these protagonists are all passionate, excessive, violent, terrible. "Doom eager," the Icelandic saga calls them. If we are meant to create in the theatre—not merely to write a well-constructed play or supply nice scenery, but to create—we shall imagine ourselves into these heroic moods. They will carry us far. For the soul is a pilgrim. If we follow it, it will lead us away from our home and into another world, a dangerous world. We shall join a band of poets and dreamers, the visionaries of the theatre: the mummers, the mountebanks, the jongleurs, the minstrels, the troubadours.

III

THE THEATRE AS IT WAS AND AS IT IS

III

THE THEATRE AS IT WAS AND AS IT IS

Magic may be real enough, the magic of word or an act, grafted upon the invisible influences that course through the material world.

—SANTAYANA

Life moves and changes and the theatre moves and changes with it. By looking at the theatre of the past, we may come to see our own theatre more clearly. The theatre of every age has something to teach us, if we are sensitive enough and humble enough to learn from it.

I am going to ask you to do the most difficult thing in the world—to imagine. Let us imagine ourselves back in the Stone Age, in the days of the cave man and the mammoth and the Altamira frescoes. It is night. We are all sitting together around a fire—Ook and Pow and Pung and Glup and Little Zowie and all the rest of us. We sit close together. We like to be together. It is safer that way, if wild beasts attack us. And besides, we are happier when we are together. We

45

are afraid to be alone. Over on that side of the fire the leaders of the tribe are sitting together—the strongest men, the men who can run fastest and fight hardest and endure longest. They have killed a lion today. We are excited about this thrilling event. We are all talking about it. We are always afraid of silence. We feel safer when somebody is talking. There is something strange about silence, strange like the black night around us, something we can never understand.

The lion's skin lies close by, near the fire. Suddenly the leader jumps to his feet. "I killed the lion! I did it! I followed him! He sprang at me! I struck at him with my spear! He fell down! He lay still!"

He is telling us. We listen. But all at once an idea comes to his dim brain. "I know a better way to tell you. See! It was like this! *Let me show you!*"

In that instant drama is born.

The leader goes on. "Sit around me in a circle —you, and you, and you—right here, where I can reach out and touch you all." And so with one inclusive gesture he makes—a theatre! From this circle of eager listeners to Reinhardt's great

Schauspielhaus in Berlin is only a step in time. In its essence a theatre is only an arrangement of seats so grouped and spaced that the actor—the leader—can reach out and touch and hold each member of his audience. Architects of later days have learned how to add convenience and comfort to this idea. But that is all. The idea itself never changes.

The leader continues: "You, Ook, over there— you stand up and be the lion. Here is the lion's skin. You put it on and be the lion and I'll kill you and we'll show them how it was." Ook gets up. He hangs the skin over his shoulders. He drops on his hands and knees and growls. How terrible he is! Of course, he isn't the real lion. We know that. The real lion is dead. We killed him today. Of course, Ook isn't a lion. Of course not. He doesn't even look like a lion. "You needn't try to scare us, Ook. We know you. We aren't afraid of you!" And yet, in some mysterious way, Ook *is* the lion. He isn't like the rest of us any longer. He is Ook all right, but he is a lion, too.

And now these two men—the world's first actors—begin to show us what the hunt was like.

They do not tell us. They *show* us. They *act* it for us. The hunter lies in ambush. The lion growls. The hunter poises his spear. The lion leaps. We all join in with yells and howls of excitement and terror—the first community chorus! The spear is thrown. The lion falls and lies still.

The drama is finished.

Now Ook takes off the lion's skin and sits beside us and is himself again. Just like you. Just like me. Good old Ook. No, not quite like you or me. Ook will be, as long as he lives, the man who can be a lion when he wants to. Pshaw! A man can't be a lion! How can a man be a lion? But Ook can make us believe it, just the same. Something queer happens to that man Ook sometimes. The lion's spirit gets into him. And we shall always look up to him and admire him and perhaps be secretly a little afraid of him. Ook is an actor. He will always be different from the rest of us, a little apart from us. For he can summon spirits.

Many thousands of years have passed since that first moment of inspiration when the theatre sprang into being. But we still like to get together, we still dread to be alone, we are still a

little awed by silence, we still like to make believe, and when an artist like Duse or Chaliapin
or Pauline Lord speaks aloud in our midst a thing
that is in the minds of all of us and fuses our various moods into one common mood, we are still
lost in wonder before this magical art of the theatre. It is really a kind of magic, this art. We call
it glamour or poetry or romance, but that doesn't
explain it. In some mysterious way these old, simple, ancestral moods still survive in us, and an
actor can make them live again for a while. We
become children once more. We believe.

Let us glance at another scene, another drama.
We are listening to the first performance of the
Antigone of Sophocles. Again I must rely on
your imagination. You have all read this play at
one time or another. You all know what Greek
actors looked like, with their masks and high
buskins. The play has been performed in your
own time and perhaps some of you have even
acted in it. But we are not in America now, and
this is not a revival. We are in a great half-circle
of stone seats built into the side of a hill. In front
of us is the stage—a long, raised platform backed

by a high screen-like wall of marble set with pillars of marble and gold. Something noble, something wonderful will presently happen on this stage. That is what it was made for. That is why we are here. It waits. We wait. We are not restless. We are content to stay in one place. Presently, in its own time, the day will come. The sun will shine upon us once more, as it has always done—the sun, too bright for our mortal eyes to look at. The sky grows lighter, but the stage is still dim and shadowy. Now the morning wind comes. We shiver a little. There is a sound of faraway doors opening "their ponderous and marble jaws." Two great dark figures steal out from opposite sides of the stage and meet in the center. They are Antigone and her sister Ismene. Their voices are lifted in a strange chant:

Do you know? Did you hear? Or have you failed to learn? . . . There is no grief, no degradation, no dishonor, not to be found among our woes. . . . What is it then?

They breathe a dreadful secret in the darkness. The first beams of the sun smite the stage. There is a fanfare of brass. The chorus enters.

Thou hast appeared at last . . . shining brighter on our seven-gated city than ever light shone before. O, eye of the day of gold!

And now the dawn has come, calm, serene, merciless as justice, inexorable as law. The drama pursues its course in the light of a new morning, marching steadily toward its climax while the sun marches steadily on toward high noon. All things are to be made clear. All things move from darkness into light. The sentence is pronounced. Antigone must go alive into the tomb. The beautiful masked figure speaks:

Men of my land, you see me taking my last walk here, looking my last upon the sunshine. Never more.

She is standing now in the shadow of the great center portal. She covers her face with her veil. Sorrow, and dread and ruin. . . . The elders of the city answer her:

And yet in glory and with praise you pass to the secret places of the dead. Alone among mankind you go to the grave alive.

Strange shadows stir in the darkness behind her. Her voice seems to come from a great distance:

I have heard of the pitiful end of the stranger from Phrygia, the daughter of Tantalus . . . most like to her, God brings me to my rest.

She speaks from another world. She is already a memory.

Cut off from friends, still living, I enter the caverned chambers of the dead. I who revered the right.

The great doors close. . . .

If we would recapture the mood of this drama today, we must turn to the music of Bach or Brahms, or to the dancing of Isadora Duncan, or to the high words of Abraham Lincoln's *Gettysburg Address:*

But, in a larger sense, we cannot dedicate, we cannot consecrate, we cannot hallow this ground . . . The world will little note, nor long remember, what we say here; but it can never forget what they did here. . . .

It is our right to be made to feel in the theatre terror and awe and majesty and rapture. But we shall not find these emotions in the theatre of today. They are not a part of our theatre any more.

Let us imagine ourselves now at the Bankside Theatre in London, in the days of Queen Elizabeth. We know today just where this theatre stood and how large it was and how it looked. Let us go there.

We are standing in the middle of a high circular building, open to the sky, with rows of balconies all around us, one above the other. At one end is the stage, a raised platform with entrances at either side and a space curtained off in the center. Above this is a balcony and above this again a kind of tower, high up against the sky. The pit where we are standing is crowded and a little dangerous. Life is cheap here at the Bankside Theatre. A stiletto under the ribs and no one is the wiser. . . . It begins to get dark. Lanterns and torches are lighted. A trumpet calls. We quiet down. High up on the platform a sentry moves—

Who's there?

Nay, stand, and unfold yourself.

We are at Elsinore. We are listening to the tragedy of *Hamlet*.

Horatio arrives with Marcellus. A bell strikes. The Ghost appears.

Nowadays, we don't believe in ghosts any more. Or at least we say we don't. But not so very many generations ago our own ancestors were burning witches for trafficking with the spirits of the dead. And I observe that when we are out in the desert, away from home, at night, sitting around a camp-fire, everyone has a mighty good ghost-story up his sleeve. And he always swears it is a true story, too. At any rate, here, in the Bankside Theatre, we do believe, and we are shaken with terror and pity at the sight of this thing out of hell. And now there is a flourish of trumpets and drums. The curtains part. The King and Queen enter in their glistering apparel, in the midst of their retinue—the counselors, the Swiss guards in bright armor, the ladies-in-waiting, the whole court of Denmark—proud, splendid, unimaginably rich in the glare of the torches. Nowadays royalty doesn't mean much in our lives. Kings and queens are curiosities, something to read about in the newspapers along with some movie Sheba's latest re-marriage. But at the Bankside, Claudius and Gertrude are literally "hedged with divinity." This very morning Queen Elizabeth herself held an audience and laid her hands on us for "king's evil," and this very afternoon we saw her go by on the Thames in her gilded barge—Elizabeth, Gloriana, Belphoebe, Star of the Sea. We know what royalty is. We have seen it. We know what great ladies and gentlemen are. We have seen them. Kings and queens and princes are all real to us; and as we watch the delicate wayward Prince Hamlet, standing there in his black, emotions of awe and affection and adoration come thronging into our minds, all blending into wonder.

What a storm of energy there is in this play! How swiftly it moves! What a rush and whirl! Now on the forestage, now on the balcony, now behind the arras, now high up on the platform. And how these players perform it! They are trained entertainers—singers, dancers, clowns—actors. Tomorrow they will do *The Merry Wives of Windsor,* and the next day Christopher Marlowe's *Tamburlane* and after that *A Midsummer*

Night's Dream or *Troilus and Cressida*. They have acted these "hits" (for that is what they are, the "hits" of their day) all over England, all over Europe. Sometimes they play before kings and queens, sometimes they play in stable-yards, before audiences of plowboys and truck drivers and sailors. They know the ways of courts and they know what it is to go hungry. They have learned their profession in a hard school of experience.

These Elizabethan actors know how to speak poetry. Hear their voices ring out in the tremendous phrases. Nowadays if we want to hear a good voice on the stage, we must go to opera. We do not expect to find one in the theatre. Music is no longer an integral part of drama. Our dramatists write for the eye, for the mind. But Shakespeare wrote for the ear. The soliloquy, "To be or not to be," is nothing more nor less than a great spoken aria. Turn to this play and read it once for the music alone.

So the drama goes on—the play, the murder, the closet-scene, the mad scene, the duel . . . mounting to its majestical end. Hamlet's body is borne to the platform. The last peal of ordnance is shot off. *The rest is silence.* . . .

And now the players are gone. What a strange thrill an empty theatre gives us! What echoes it carries, and what memories! Here was a dream, a high, swift, passionate, terrible dream. We have been brought face to face with the majesty and splendor of destiny. *Perhaps all the sins and energies of the world are only the world's flight from an infinite blinding beam.*

In the early days of the eighteenth century an English playwright named William Congreve wrote a comedy which he called *The Way of the World*. Let us go to London to see this play.

We are in a great hall lighted by crystal chandeliers. How did the drama get indoors? Nobody seems to know. The thing that is going to happen in this playhouse is neither religious ritual nor great popular art. There is a feeling of privacy here. A curtain covers one end of the room. A curtain . . . ? What is behind it? Something intimate, something personal, something . . . a little indiscreet? perhaps . . . Congreve will tell us. A servant trims the candles that burn in a row at the foot of the curtain. There is a preluding of fiddles. The curtain is lifted. We look at a room that is not a real room, but a kind of thin, delicate, exaggerated echo of a room, all painted on screens of canvas. The actors enter, each one bowing to the audience. They look like nothing human, like nothing ever seen on this earth. The ladies' cheeks are rouged with a high hectic red. They wear frail iridescent dresses of silk and lace. They are laden with jewels. They carry masks and fans. The men wear periwigs and rapiers. Their heels click on the polished floors. Their hands are covered with long lace ruffles and they glitter with diamonds. The sense of luxury has come into the theatre. The players float and waver in the warm air that streams up from the tapers, like butterflies, like ephemera, born to shine a moment for our pleasure, for our humor, for our distinguished indulgence. *Et puis—bon soir!* Life? Don't come too near it! Life is just something that effervesces for a moment and goes flat. Life is a nuance, a gesture, a flicker . . . rouge . . . blood . . . ashes. . . . Love? Whoever said there was such a thing as love in the world? We know better. But while we are here we will keep up the show. And a brave show it is, a dazzling show. Distinguished manners, effrontery, phrases like fireworks. . . . But here comes Mistress

Millamant, i'faith, full sail, with her fan spread and her streamers out, and a shoal of fools for tenders:

You seem to be unattended, Madam—you used to have the beau monde throng after you; and a flock of gay fine perukes hovering round you.

O, I have denied myself airs today, I have walked as fast through the crowd—

As a favorite just disgraced; and with as few followers.

Dear Mr. Witwoud, truce with your similitudes; for I am as sick of 'em—

As a physician of a good air.—I cannot help it, Madam, though 'tis against myself.

Yet, again!—Mincing, stand between me and his wit.

Do, Mrs. Mincing, like a screen before a great fire.—I confess I do blaze today, I am too bright.

Flutes and hautboys in the air around us. . . .
There is a remarkable actress in London, Miss Edith Evans, who can speak lines like these with the precision and variety of a Heifetz. It is a very special pleasure to listen to her, and you have only to hear her go through an act of *The*

Beaux' Stratagem to realize that she has perfected an art of musical speaking that is almost unknown in our day. When a playwright begins to awaken the music that lies in the spoken word, and when an actor begins to give this music its value, a new theatre springs into being.

Plot? Oh, yes, to be sure, there is a plot. But if it should ever chance to obtrude itself too much, someone on the stage will cry out, "Come, I have a song for you, and I see one in the next room who will sing it."

And then Congreve will carelessly toss us an incomparable lyric like this:

I tell thee, Charmian, could I time retrieve,
And once again begin to love and live,
To you I should my earliest offering give;

I know my eyes would lead my heart to you,
And I should all my vows and hopes renew;
But to be plain, I never would be true. . . .

There is a moral lesson in this play, too, thrown in for good measure. Certainly, there is a moral lesson. Virtue triumphs in the end, as virtue should. But we shall not take it too seriously. It is all a part of the graceful ephemeral dance.

The epilogue is spoken. The players bow themselves out in a minuet. We shall meet them a little later in the evening at one of the fashionable chocolate-houses. *As for living, our servants can do that for us,* a Frenchman said, a century and a half later.

Somewhere around 1840 a very strange thing happens. A man named David Hill discovers how to make a thing he calls a photograph. It is a picture made on a sensitive plate of metal by rays of light, a picture of things exactly as they are. All art is profoundly influenced by this discovery. We all become fascinated by actuality. We want to see everything just as it is. We want people on the stage to walk and talk just as they do off the stage. Soon afterward the first real Brussels carpet makes its appearance in the theatre. Scene-painting becomes realistic, acting becomes casual, dialogue is modeled after the speech of everyday life. Let us drop in at a performance of Ibsen's *Hedda Gabler* in the early '90's.

The curtain goes up. We are looking at a room. At first glance it seems just like a real room with one wall taken off. It is a tasteful, agreeable room, furnished, exactly as a real room would be, with tables and chairs and sofas and bric-a-brac. We might have taken tea here this very afternoon. This room has been lived in. It has an atmosphere. We can tell what the people who live here are like. The room has taken on something of their quality, just as an old coat gets molded to the person who wears it, and keeps the impress of his body afterward. See, there is General Gabler's portrait in the room beyond, and there are his pistols on the old piano, and the room is filled with flowers, and over there is a stove with a fire in it.

The play begins. How odd! Here is no solemn public ritual, no spoken opera, but a kind of betrayal. We are all eavesdroppers, peering through a keyhole, minding other people's business. We look in at the private affairs of the Tesmans, and we listen to them with the same eager, shocked, excited interest with which we might read the details of some court-room revelation. We see a spoiled, hysterical woman, dressed in the latest fashions from Paris. She pokes fun at Aunt Julia's bonnet. She pulls Mrs. Elvsted's hair. She burns Lovborg's manuscript. She is going to have a baby and she doesn't want it. She plays the piano and shoots herself. The characters talk like this:

Well, well, then . . . My hat—? My over-coat—? Oh, in the hall— I do hope I shan't come too late, Hedda! Eh? . . . Oh, if you run—

and

Mrs. Elvsted. . . . Oh, yes, Sheriff Elvsted's wife . . . Miss Rysing that was . . . that girl with the irritating hair that she was always show-ing off . . . an old flame of yours, someone told me. . . .

It is all given to us in the language of everyday life. Just like a living picture. We might be lis-tening to people on the street. . . . Little by little we become aware of a strange deep tragic play and interplay of motives behind the conven-tional surface. We are overcome by an inescapable sense of fatality. The ancient terror spreads its shadow over the drama. The pistol-shot at the end is the finale of a great tragic symphony.

And here we are back again. Our theatre is concerned with Little Theatre Movements and talking pictures and censorship and unions and interlocking dimmer-boxes. Fashions change. In *Uncle Tom's Cabin,* written not so long ago, little Eva's father clasps her to his heart and murmurs:

O Evangeline, rightly named? Thou art indeed an Evangel to me!

In Maurice Watkin's *Chicago,* a sensational success in New York, the show-girl heroine yells:

You Goddamned louse!

and drops her man with a pearl-handled revolver. Fashions do, indeed, change. We are not living in the Stone Age any more, nor the time of the Renaissance, nor the time of the Restoration, nor in the Mauve Decade. These are the days of the candid camera and the comic strip and television and reducing diets and strange new dance-steps. We have to work in the theatre of our own time with the tools of our own time. . . . I will tell you now why I have made these images of the theatre of other days. In all these dramas of the past there is a dream—an excitement, a high, rare mood, a conception of greatness. If we are to create in the theatre, we must bring back this mood, this excitement, this dream. The plain truth is that life has become so crowded, so hurried, so commonplace, so ordinary, that we have lost the artist's approach to art. Without this, we are nothing. With this, everything is possible. Here it is, in these old dramas. Let us see it. Let us learn it. Let us bring into the theatre a vision of what the theatre might be. There is no other way. Indeed, there is no other way.

IV

TO A YOUNG STAGE DESIGNER

IV

TO A YOUNG STAGE DESIGNER

Beauty is the purgation of superfluities.
—MICHELANGELO

Behind the words and movements, imperturbable,
withdrawn, slumbered a strange smoldering power.
—HENRY BROCKEN

A STAGE DESIGNER is, in a very real sense, a jack-of-all-trades. He can make blueprints and murals and patterns and light-plots. He can design fireplaces and bodices and bridges and wigs. He understands architecture, but is not an architect: can paint a portrait, but is not a painter: creates costumes, but is not a couturier. Although he is able to call upon any or all of these varied gifts at will, he is not concerned with any one of them to the exclusion of the others, nor is he interested in any one of them for its own sake. These talents are only the tools of his trade. His real calling is something quite different. He is *an artist of occasions.*

Every play—or rather, every performance of a play—is an occasion, and this occasion has its own characteristic quality, its own atmosphere, so to speak. It is the task of the stage designer to enhance and intensify this characteristic quality by every means in his power. The mastery of this special art demands not only a mastery of many diverse techniques but a temperament that is peculiarly sensitive to the atmosphere of a given occasion, just as the temperament of a musician is peculiarly sensitive to the characteristic qualities of a musical composition. Stage designers, like musicians, are born and not made. One is aware of atmospheres or one isn't, just as one has a musical ear or one hasn't.

A stage setting has no independent life of its own. Its emphasis is directed toward the performance. In the absence of the actor it does not exist. Strange as it may seem, this simple and fundamental principle of stage design still seems to be widely misunderstood. How often in critics' reviews one comes upon the phrase "the settings were gorgeous!" Such a statement, of course, can mean only one thing, that no one concerned with producing the drama has thought of it as an organic whole. I quote from a review recently published in one of our leading newspapers, "Of all the sets of the season, the only true scenic surprise was . . ." The only true scenic surprise, indeed! Every stage designer worth his salt outgrew the idea of scenic surprises years ago. If the critics only knew how easy it is to make a scenic surprise in the theatre! Take two turntables, a great deal of— But, no. Why give away the formula? It is not surprise that is wanted from the audience; it is delighted and trusting acceptance. The surprise inherent in a stage setting is only a part of the greater surprise inherent in the event itself.

And yet a stage setting holds a curious kind of suspense. Go, for instance, into an ordinary empty drawing-room as it exists normally. There is no particular suspense about this room. It is just— empty. Now imagine the same drawing-room arranged and decorated for a particular function—a Christmas party for children, let us say. It is not completed as a room, now, until the children are in it. And if we wish to visualize for ourselves how important a part the sense of expectancy plays in such a room, let us imagine that there is a storm and that the children cannot come. A scene on the stage is filled with the same feeling of expectancy. It is like a mixture of chemical elements held in solution. The actor adds the one element that releases the hidden energy of the whole. Meanwhile, wanting the actor, the various elements which go to make up the setting remain suspended, as it were, in an indefinable tension. To create this suspense, this tension, is the essence of the problem of stage designing.

The designer must strive to achieve in his settings what I can only call a high potential. The walls, the furniture, the properties, are only the facts of a setting, only the outline. The truth is in everything but these objects, in the space they enclose, in the intense vibration they create. They are fused into a kind of embodied impulse. When the curtain rises we feel a frenzy of excitement focused like a burning-glass upon the actors. Everything on the stage becomes a part of the life of the instant. The play becomes a voice out of a whirlwind. The terrible and wonderful *dynamis* of the theatre pours over the footlights.

A strange, paradoxical calling, to work always behind and around, to bring into being a powerful non-being. How far removed it all is from the sense of display! One is reminded of the portraits of the Spanish noblemen painted by El Greco in the Prado in Madrid, whose faces, as Arthur Symons said, are all nerves, distinguished nerves, quieted by an effort. What a phrase for stage designers to remember! *Quieted by an effort.* . . .

It is to the credit of our designers that they have almost made a fetish of abnegation. But let me remark parenthetically that it is sometimes difficult to go into the background when there is nothing in front of you. These pages are hardly the place in which to perpetuate the centuries-old squabble between playwrights and stage designers begun by peevish old Ben Jonson, who scolded Inigo Jones so roundly for daring to make his productions beautiful and exciting to look at. This kind of petty jealousy makes sorry reading even when recorded in verse by the great Ben himself. It is enough to say that the jealousy still persists and is as corroding in the twentieth century as it was in the seventeenth. The error lies in our conception of the theatre as something set aside for talents that are purely literary. As if the experience of the theatre had only to do with words! Our playwrights need to learn that plays are wrought, not written. There is something to be said in the theatre in terms of form and color and light that can be said in no other way.

The designer must learn to sense the atmosphere of a play with unusual clearness and exactness. He must actually live in it for a time, immerse himself in it, be baptized by it. This process is by no means so easy as it seems. We are all too apt to substitute ingenuity for clairvoyance. The temptation to invent is always present. I was once asked to be one of the judges of a competition of stage designs held by the Department of Drama of one of our well-known universities. All the designers had made sketches for the same play. The setting was the interior of a peasant hut on the west coast of Ireland. It turned out that these twenty or thirty young designers had mastered the technique of using dimmers and sliding stages and projected scenery. They had also acquired a considerable amount of information concerning the latest European developments of stagecraft. Their drawings were full of expressionism from Germany, constructivism from Russia, every kind of modernism. They were compilations of everything that had been said and done in the world of scenery in the last twenty years. But not one of the designers had sensed the atmosphere of the particular play in question.

I recalled for them my memory of the setting for the same play as produced by the Abbey Theatre on its first visit to America. This setting was very simple, far simpler and far less self-conscious than any of their designs. Neutral-tinted walls, a fireplace, a door, a window, a table, a few chairs, the red homespun skirts and bare feet of the peasant girls. A fisher's net, perhaps. Nothing more. But through the little window at the back one saw a sky of enchantment. All the poetry of Ireland shone in that little square of light, moody, haunting, full of dreams, calling us to follow on, follow on. . . . By this one gesture of excelling simplicity the setting was enlarged into the region of great theatre art.

Now here is a strange thing, I said to the designers. If we can succeed in seeing the essential quality of a play others will see it, too. We know the truth when we see it, Emerson said, from opinion, as we know that we are awake when we are awake. For example: you have never been in Heaven, and you have never seen an angel. But if someone produces a play about angels whose scenes are laid in Heaven you will know at a glance whether his work is right or wrong. Some curious intuition will tell you. The sense of recognition is the highest experience the theatre can give. As we work we must seek not for self-expression or for performance for its own sake, but only to establish the dramatist's intention, knowing that when we have succeeded in doing so audiences will say to themselves, not, This is beautiful, This is charming, This is splendid, but —This is true. This is the way it is. So it is, and not otherwise. . . . There is nothing esoteric in the search for truth in the theatre. On the contrary, it is a part of the honest everyday life of the theatre.

The energy of a particular play, its emotional content, its aura, so to speak, has its own definite physical dimensions. It extends just so far in space and no farther. The walls of the setting must be placed at precisely this point. If the setting is larger than it should be, the audience gets a feeling of meagerness and hollowness; if smaller, a feeling of confusion and pressure. It is often very difficult to adjust the physical limits of a setting to its emotional limitations. But great plays exist outside the categories of dimension. Their bounty is as boundless as the air. Accordingly we need not think of a stage-setting, in a larger sense, as a matter of establishing space relations. Great plays have nothing to do with space. The setting for a great play is no more subject to the laws of space composition than music is. We may put aside once and for all the idea of a stage-setting as a glorified show-window in which actors are to be exhibited and think of it instead as a kind of symphonic accompaniment or obbligato to the play, as evocative and intangible as music itself. Indeed, music may play a more important role than we now realize in the scenic evocations of the future.

In the last analysis the designing of stage scenery is not the problem of an architect or a painter or a sculptor or even a musician, but of a poet. By a poet I do not mean, of course, an artist who is concerned only with the writing of verse. I am speaking of the poetic attitude. The recognized poet, Stedman says, is one who gives voice in expressive language to the common thought and feeling which lie deeper than ordinary speech. I will give you a very simple illustration. Here is a fragment of ordinary speech, a paraphrase of part of Hamlet's soliloquy, *To be or not to be:*

I wish I were dead! I wish I could go to sleep and never wake up! But I'm afraid of what might happen afterward. Do people dream after they are dead? . . . But Hamlet does not express himself in this way. He says, *To die, to sleep; to sleep: perchance to dream: ay, there's the rub; for in that sleep of death what dreams may come.* . . . Here are two ways of saying the same thing. The first is prose. The second is poetry. Both of them are true. But Shakespeare's way—the poetic way—is somehow deeper and higher and truer and more universal. In this sense we may fairly speak of the art of stage designing as poetic, in that it seeks to give expression to the essential quality of a play rather than to its outward characteristics.

Some time ago one of the younger stage designers was working with me on the scenes for an historical play. In the course of the production we had to design a tapestry, which was to be decorated with figures of heraldic lions. I sent him to the library to hunt up old documents. He came back presently with many sketches, copies of originals. They were all interesting enough, but somehow they were not right. They lacked something that professionals call "good theatre."

They were not *theatrical*. They were accurate and
—lifeless. I said as much to the designer. "Well,
what shall we do about it?" he asked me. "We
have got to stop copying," I said. "We must try
something else. We must put our imaginations
to work. Let us think now. Not about what this
heraldic lion ought to look like, but what the design meant in the past, in the Middle Ages.

"Perhaps Richard, the Lion-Heart, carried this
very device emblazoned on his banner as he
marched across Europe on his way to the Holy
Land. Richard, the Lion-Heart, *Coeur de Lion*
. . . What memories of childhood this name con-
jures up, what images of chivalry! Knights in
armor, enchanted castles, magic casements, peril-
ous seas, oriflammes, and gonfalons. Hear the
great battle-cries! See the banners floating
through the smoke! *Coeur de Lion,* the Cru-
sader, with his singing page Blondel. . . . Do
you remember Blondel's song, the song he sang
for three long years while he sought his master
in prison? *'O Richard, O mon Roi! L'Univers
t'abandonne! . . .'*

"And now your imagination is free to wander,
if you will allow it to do so, among the great
names of romance. Richard, the Lion-Heart,

King Arthur, Sir Percival and the mystery of the Holy Grail, the Song of Roland, the magic sword, Durandal, Tristan and Isolde, the love-potion, the chant of the Cornish sailors, the ship with the black sail; the Lady Nicolette of whom Aucassin said, *Beau venir et bel aller,* lovely when you come, lovely when you go; the demoiselle Aude, who died for love; the Lady Christabel; the Ancient Mariner with the Albatross hung about his neck; the Cid, Charlemagne, Barbarossa, the Tartar, Kubla Khan, who decreed the pleasure-dome in Xanadu, in the poem Coleridge heard in a dream. . . . And there are the legendary cities, too, Carcassonne, Granada, Torcello; Samarkand, the Blue City, with its façades of turquoise and lapis lazuli; Carthage, Isfahan, Trebizond; and there are the places which have never existed outside a poet's imagination— Hy Brasil, Brocéliande, the Land of Luthany, the region Elenore, the Isle of Avalon, *where falls not hail, or rain, or any snow, where ever King Arthur lyeth sleeping as in peace.* . . . And there is the winged Lion of St. Mark in Venice with the device set forth fairly beneath it, *Pax Tibi, Marce, Evangelista Meus;* and there are the mounted knights in the windows of Chartres,

riding on, riding on toward Our Lady as she
bends above the high altar in her glory of rose.

"These images of romance have come to our
minds—all of them—out of this one little symbol
of the heraldic lion. They are dear to us. They
can never fade from our hearts.

"Let your fancy dwell and move among them
in a kind of revery. Now, in this mood, with
these images bright in your mind, draw your
figure of the lion once more.

"This new drawing is different. Instead of
imitating, describing what the artists of the Middle Ages thought a lion looked like, it summons
up an image of medieval romance. Perhaps without knowing it I have stumbled on a definition of
art in the theatre; all art in the theatre should be,
not descriptive, but evocative. Not a description,
but an evocation. A bad actor describes a character; he explains it. He expounds it. A good actor
evokes a character. He summons it up. He re-
veals it to us. . . . This drawing is evocative.
Something about it brings back memories of
medieval love-songs and crusaders and high adventures. People will look at it without knowing
why. In this drawing of a lion—only a detail in
a magnificent, elaborate setting—there will be a

quality which will attract them and disturb them and haunt them and make them dream. Your feeling is in it. Your interest is in it. You have triumphed over the mechanics of the theatre and for the time being you have become a poet."

The poetic conception of stage design bears little relation to the accepted convention of realistic scenery in the theatre. As a matter of fact it is quite the opposite. Truth in the theatre, as the masters of the theatre have always known, stands above and beyond mere accuracy to fact. In the theatre the actual thing is never the exciting thing. Unless life is turned into art on the stage it stops being alive and goes dead.

So much for the realistic theatre. *The artist should omit the details, the prose of nature and give us only the spirit and splendor.* When we put a star in a sky, for example, it is not just a star in a sky, but a "supernal messenger, excellently bright." This is purely a question of our point of view. A star is, after all, only an electric light. The point is, how the audience will see it, what images it will call to mind. We read of Madame Pitoeff's Ophelia that in the Mad Scene she handled the roses and the rosemary and the rue as if she were in a Paradise of flowers.

We must bring into the immediate life of the theatre—"the two hours' traffic of our stage"—images of a larger life. The stage we inhabit is a chamber of the House of Dreams. Our work on this stage is to suggest the immanence of a visionary world all about us. In this world Hamlet dwells, and Oedipus, and great Juno, known by her immortal gait, and the three witches on the blasted heath. We must learn by a deliberate effort of the will to walk in these enchanted regions. We must imagine ourselves into their vastness.

Here is the secret of the flame that burns in the work of the great artists of the theatre. They seem so much more aware than we are, and so much more awake, and so much more alive that they make us feel that what we call living is not living at all, but a kind of sleep. Their knowledge, their wealth of emotion, their wonder, their elation, their swift clear seeing surrounds every occasion with a crowd of values that enriches it beyond anything which we, in our happy satisfaction, had ever imagined. In their hands it becomes not only a thing of beauty but a thing of power. And we see it all—beauty and power alike—as a part of the life of the theatre.

V

SOME THOUGHTS ON STAGE COSTUME

V

SOME THOUGHTS ON STAGE COSTUME

Let us have a glimpse of incomprehensibles: and thoughts of things, which thoughts but tenderly touch.

—SIR THOMAS BROWNE

IN LEARNING how a costume for the stage is designed and made, we have to go through a certain amount of routine training. We must learn about patterns, and about periods. We have to know what farthingales are, and wimples, and patches and calèches and parures and godets and appliqués and passementerie. We have to know the instant we see and touch a fabric what it will look like on the stage both in movement and in repose. We have to develop the brains that are in our fingers. We have to enhance our feeling for style in the theatre. We have to experiment endlessly until our work is as nearly perfect as we can make it, until we are, so to speak, released from it. All this is a part of our apprenticeship. But there comes to every one of us a time when the problem of creating presents itself.

If we are to accomplish anything in any art we must first see what our problem is before we can proceed to solve it. What we do in the theatre depends upon what we see. If we are to design for the theatre we must have the clearest possible image in our minds of the nature and the purpose and the function of the theatre.

Now this theatre we are working in is a very strange place. It deals, not with logic, but with magic. It deals with witchcraft and demoniac possession and forebodings and ecstasies and mystical splendors and legends and playthings and parades and suspicions and mysteries and rages and jealousies and unleashed passions and thrilling intimations and austerity and elevation and luxury and ruin and woe and exaltation and secrets "too divinely precious not to be forbidden," —the shudder, the frisson, the shaft of chill moonlight, the footfall on the stair, the knife in the heart, the face at the window, the boy's hand on the hill. . . . The air of the theatre is filled with extravagant and wheeling emotions, with what H. L. Mencken calls "the grand crash and glitter of things."

In the theatre, the supernormal is the only norm and anything less is subnormal, devitalized.

If we try to bring the theatre down to our own level, it simply ceases to be. When we see *Oedipus Rex* in the theatre, when we hear *Pelléas and Mélisande,* when we examine a stage design by Adolphe Appia, we realize that great artists like Sophocles and Debussy and Appia create as they do, not only because they are more skilled, more experienced than the rest of us, but because they think and feel differently from the way the rest of us do. Their orientation is different from our own. When we listen to what artists tell us in their work—when we look at what they look at and try to see what they see—then, and only then, do we learn from them.

There is no formula for inspiration. But to ask ourselves, why did that artist do that thing in that particular way instead of in some other way? is to take the first step toward true creation.

Nature has endowed us all with a special faculty called imagination, by means of which we can form mental images of things not present to our senses. Trevisa, a seer of the late fourteenth century, defined it as the faculty whereby "the soul beholds the likeness of things that be absent." It is the most precious, the most powerful, and the most unused of all human faculties. Like the mantle of rainbow feathers in the Japanese No drama, *Hagoromo,* it is a treasure not lightly given to mortals. Many people confuse imagination with ingenuity, with inventiveness. But imagination is not this thing at all. It is the peculiar power of seeing with the eye of the mind. And it is the very essence of the theatre.

Many of you are familiar with the region of the Ardennes, in Belgium. Now this countryside, charming and poignant though it is, may seem no more beautiful than many parts of our own country, nearer and dearer to us. But Shakespeare once went there. And in his drama, *As You Like It,* the familiar scene is no longer the Ardennes we know, but the Forest of Arden, where on every enchanted tree hang the tongues that show the beauties of Orlando's Rosalind.

Atalanta's better part, sad Lucretia's modesty.

Shakespeare's imagination joins with our own to summon up an ideal land, an image of our lost paradise. Or let us take another example: King Lear had, I dare say, a life of his own outside the limits of Shakespeare's play, a daily life of routine very much like our own. He got up in the morning and put on his boots and ate his breakfast and signed dull documents and yawned and grumbled and was bored like everyone else in the world. But the drama does not give us those moments. It gives us Lear at his highest pitch of living. It shows him in intensest action, a wild old man storming at heaven, bearing his daughter Cordelia, dead in his arms.

In these examples we may divine Shakespeare's own intention toward the theatre. His attitude— the true dramatic attitude, the mood, indeed, in which all great art is created—is one of intense awareness, of infectious excitement. If we are to create in the theatre, we must first learn to put on this creative intention like the mantle of rainbow feathers. We must learn to feel the drive and beat of the dramatic imagination in its home. We must take the little gift we have into the hall of the gods.

A stage costume is a creation of the theatre. Its quality is purely theatrical and taken outside the theatre, it loses its magic at once. It dies as a plant dies when uprooted. Why this should be so I do not know. But here is one more proof of the eternal enchantment which every worker in the theatre knows and feels. The actual materials of which a stage costume is made count for very little. Outwardly it may be nothing more than an arrangement of shabby velvets and cheap glass "glits." I remember Graham-Robertson's description of a costume worn by Ellen Terry as *Fair Rosamund:*

> *She looked her loveliest in the rich gown of her first entrance, a wonderful Rosettian effect of soft gold and glowing color veiled in black, her masses of bright hair in a net of gold and golden hearts embroidered on her robe. . . . The foundation was an old pink gown, worn with stage service and reprieved for the occasion from the rag-bag. The mysterious veiling was the coarsest and cheapest black net, the glory of hair through golden meshes was a bag of gold tinsel stuffed with crumpled paper, and the broidered hearts were cut out of gold paper and gummed on. The whole costume would have been dear at ten shillings and was one of the finest stage dresses that I have ever seen.*

The wardrobes of our costume-establishments are crammed with hundreds of just such costumes. I can see them now, with their gilt and their fustian and their tinsel and their bands of sham ermine. You all know them—the worn hems, the sleeves shortened and lengthened and shortened again, the seams taken in and let out and taken in, the faded tights, the embroidery hastily freshened with new bits from the stockroom, the fashions of yesterday gone flat like stale champagne. . . . But in the theatre a miracle takes place. The dramatic imagination transforms them. They become dynamic. They become a surprise, an adventure, a reminder of things we once knew and now remember with joy. The actors wearing them become ambassadors from that bright other world behind the footlights.

But a stage costume has an added significance in the theatre in that it is created to enhance the particular quality of a special occasion. It is designed for a particular character in a particular scene in a particular play—not just for a character in a scene in a play, but for *that* character, in *that* scene, in *that* play—and accordingly it is an organic and necessary part of the drama in which it appears. One might say that an ordinary costume, an ordinary suit or dress, is an organic and necessary part of our everyday living. And so it is. But—and here is the point!—drama is not everyday living. Drama and life are two very different things. Life, as we all live it, is made up of troubles and blunders and dreams that are never fully realized. "The eternal ever-not-quite," William James called it. We go on from day to day, most of us, beset by uncertainties and frustrations, and try to do the best we can, not seeing very clearly, not understanding very well. And we say, Life is like that! But drama is not in the least like that. Drama is life, to be sure, but life seen through the eye of a dramatist, seen sharply and together, and given an arbitrary form and order. We see our own lives reflected as in a magic mirror, enlarged and simplified, in a pattern we had not perceived before. Everything on his stage becomes a part of that other order—the words, the situations, the actors, the setting, the lights, the costumes. Each element has its own particular relation to the drama and plays its own part in the drama. And each element—the word, the actor, the costume—has the exact significance of a note in a symphony. Each separate costume we create for a play must be exactly suited both to the character it helps to express and to the occasion it graces. We shall not array Lady Macbeth in pale blue organdie or Ariel in purple velvet. Mephistopheles will wear his scarlet and Hamlet his solemn black as long as the theatre continues to exist. A Hamlet in real life may possess a wardrobe of various styles and colors. But in the theatre it is simply not possible for Mr. John Gielgud or Mr. Maurice Evans to say, *'Tis not alone my tawny cloak, good mother, nor customary suits of tender green. . . .*

With these two essentials of stage costume in mind—theatricality and appropriateness—let us consider a particular illustration of the problem of costume designing. I have purposely chosen an example that is as remote as possible from our everyday experience, in order that it may give more scope for our imaginations. Let us go back three hundred years in history, to another theatre altogether. John Milton wrote a poetic tragedy, *Samson Agonistes,* thought by many to be the most sublime example of drama in this or any language. As we read this tragedy, we presently come upon the following curiously evocative passage of description:

But who is this, what thing of Sea or Land?
Female of sex it seems,
That so bedeckt, ornate, and gay,
Comes this way sailing

Like a stately ship
Of Tarsus, bound for th' Isles
Of Javan or Gadier
With all her bravery on, and tackle trim,
Sails fill'd, and streamers waving,
Courted by all the winds that hold them play,
An amber scent of odorous perfume
Her Harbinger . . .

Here is an example of the dramatic imagination in action, full blown, at the top of its bent. This Titan among dreamers, the man who could write lines like *And now on earth the seventh evening arose in Eden,* is describing a costume. A stage costume, if you please. Let us try to visualize this costume.

Fortunately we all have—or at least we ought to have—a reasonably clear idea of what a woman's costume looked like in Milton's day. We have all seen pictures of the tight bodices and the full stiff skirts and the ruffs and the jewels. And we can find plenty of documents, if we need them, on the shelves of our libraries. But documents will not help us here, or at most they will serve only as a starting-point from which to proceed. What we are after at the moment is not erudition, but evocation. We are to evoke a mental image of this costume. We are to allow it to appear to us of itself, to manifest itself to us, to occur to us, as it were. We shall find this exercise a difficult one, entirely outside of our usual routine, but in the end strangely rewarding. We shall discover that our imagination possesses a curious focusing and projecting power. I have often inquired in vain as to the precise nature of this visioning faculty. Does the costume we are about to discuss already exist in some ideal platonic world of images? Have our imaginations bodies? I do not know. I only know that this faculty of strong inward viewing functions in accordance with an old, old law. I cannot pretend to explain it. I can only affirm it. It simply is so. Perhaps this is what Leonardo da Vinci had in mind when he declared that the human eye not only receives but projects rays of light.

Our first step is to visualize this costume in relation to Milton's own time. We know that the costumes of any period in history are typical of that period. For example, let us think of the costumes of today in relation to the life of today. Here are a few catchwords chosen almost at random out of the daily papers: television, airplane, jitterbug, streamline, New Deal, A. F. of L., C.I.O., C.C.C., P.W.A. And so on. As we read them we instantly get an impression—broad, general, rough, to be sure, but still an impression —of the characteristic quality of our own epoch, swift, direct, inclusive, brilliant, staccato. Now what could be more expressive of this quality than the snappy chic nervous little tailored suits we see by the dozens in our fashion magazines and in our shop windows? Look at the tight little sweaters and coats and skirts and the closely wrapped turbans, all so simple and practical, all made, not to charm, but to surprise and excite, all like quick bold sketches, to be rubbed out to-morrow. They are creations of—and for—this unique moment in time. Seen in retrospect, they may give the historians of the future as clear an idea of this particular era in the world's history as a sixteen-millimeter camera or the Grand Coulee Dam. They are an inseparable part of our own special idiom.

In the same way a costume of Milton's own time will inevitably express the characteristic qualities of life at that time. Let us bring to mind what we know of these qualities. Great names rise in the memory: England: Elizabeth the

Queen, the sovereign who once said, I could have wept but that my face was made for the day: Sir Francis Drake, the defeat of the Spanish Armada, the streets of London all hung with blue, like the sea: William Shakespeare, author and player, the greatest master of public art the world has ever known: Marlowe, with his "mighty line"— Kit Marlowe, stabbed in the Mermaid Tavern in Southwark over across the bridge; Sir Walter Raleigh, with his cloak and his sea-knowledge and his new colony, Virginia, in the west, on the other side of the world; Spenser and Sir Philip Sidney, Ben Jonson, Inigo Jones; Bacon, Leicester, Essex: Mary of Scotland, whose skin was so fair, men said, that when she drank red wine you could see the red drops running down in her throat like fire. . . . These names out of history, stirring, blood-swept, passionate, mingle and blend in our minds in an overpowering sense of splendor and reckless adventure and incredible energy and high fantastical dreams. And then we see John Bunyan's Christian, accompanied by Ignorance and Faith and Hope and Mistrust, on his way to the Celestial City, his soul intent on cherubim and seraphim. And Sir Thomas Browne admonishes us in his echoing cadences to be ready to be anything in the ecstasy of being ever. And we hear John Milton as he dictates the "Sonnet on His Blindness"—*God doth not need either man's work or His own gifts.* The Reformation is here, with its fervors and its exaltations and its solemn preoccupations with moral grandeur.

As we dwell upon these things, the dramatic imagination begins to sketch in our minds the first vague outlines of a costume. It is bold and fantastic and elaborate and ceremonious and splendid, a typical expression of the Age of Daring. So much we see. Let us pause for a moment and consider the costume from another point of view, this time in relation to the quality of Milton's own poetry. The chief trait of any given poet, Walt Whitman reminds us, is always the mood out of which he contemplates his subjects. Milton's mood is mature, noble, grand. His season is autumn, splendid and serene, a "season of mellow fruitfulness." And we find in his poetry a great elegance, a slightly rigid elegance perhaps, like the elegance which is at times almost a constraint in the music of Handel or Purcell. It is often gay, jocund, buxom, one might say; hearty, with a great natural health coursing through it; but it is never merely funny, as Will Shakespeare is funny, for instance, when he makes Juliet's Nurse say, *Now, afore God, I am so vexed that every part about me quivers.* Nothing so frivolous here. Milton's verse is all in the noble heroic vein, in the Dorian mode. It is ordered, splendid, a great pavane, a gorgeous pageant, a concert of organ and orchestra led by a master of sound. It is laid out like a formal garden, all glowing in autumn sunlight, along whose enchanted avenues we may wander for hours. Until the tempest comes, and lightning splits the sky, and the earth reels, and we hear the voices in heaven chanting, *Of Man's first disobedience and the Fruit.*

In the light of these "solemn planetary wheelings" our imaginary costume takes on new qualities. It is more triumphant, more astonishing, than we had originally thought. But there is a certain elegant sobriety about it which we had not sensed at first. It is a Miltonian costume, the creation of an adult mind.

Let us imagine that we see it in its own proper surroundings. It is a stage costume; let us see it on a stage, then—in Whitehall, perhaps, or in one of the theatres designed by Inigo Jones. A figure appears before us like something seen between sleeping and waking, or in a daydream, vague, arresting, unfamiliar. It moves in a quivering amber twilight, a romantic dusk made by hundreds of tiny tapers placed about the proscenium. You will note that our imaginary Miltonian theatre has not the benefit of our modern mechanisms for lighting the stage, our Leicas and Fresnels and interlocking dimmer-boxes. Yet the old theatre lighting, in spite of its crudeness, had a quality which our modern lighting sadly lacks, a quality which I can only describe as *dreaminess*. Our plays are case-histories, not dreams, and for the most part they are played in the pitiless light that beats down upon an operating table. But in that low shadowless amber radiance the unusual, the extraordinary, the fabulous, came into its own.

Accordingly the stage costumes of those times were made to catch and drink up every stray wandering beam of light and reflect it back to the audience. They gleam and flash and glitter. *Glister* is the real word. They sparkle and twinkle and blaze with gold and silver and color and spangles and jewels. They transform the actor into a being of legend.

We have examined our costume in the light—figuratively speaking—of the wonderful period in history we call the Reformation, and in the light of Milton's own solemn poetic imagery. We see that it has—indeed, that it must have—the qualities of boldness, fantasy, dignity, formality. Now, as we look at it in the light of the theatre of that earlier day, we add to it the qualities of glamour and luster. Step by step it becomes clearer in our minds. It becomes iridescent, becomes radiant. It glows and shines.

And now let us be specific, and ask in Milton's own words, *But who is this?*

It is Delilah, the wife of Samson, the woman whom he knew and loved in the valley of Sorek. This curious figure, this living shell, this incredible puppet encased in its elaborate dress, so stiff it almost stands alone, is Delilah. In the argument of the sixteenth chapter of Judges we may read her story:

Delilah, corrupted by the Philistines, enticeth Samson. Thrice she is deceived. At last she overcometh him. The Philistines take him and put out his eyes. His strength recovering, he pulleth down the house upon the Philistines, and dieth.

We are apt to look at such a story today too exclusively from an analytic point of view. We

take the cue from our doctors of psychology, with
their flair for definition, and we call Delilah a
vampire, or an anima-figure, it may be. Or we
take the cue from Kipling and think sentimen-
tally of a fool and a rag and a bone and a hank of
hair. Or we take the cue from Hollywood and
call Delilah simply "the menace." The fact is,
however, that in so doing we divest the story of
the emotional values that have crowded about it
ever since our infancy. We analyze it, delimit it,
and dismiss it from our minds. But it is precisely
these emotional values that should interest us
most. Our aim here is to recapture our childhood
memories and the mood they bring with them,
the atmosphere of nobility and betrayal and
vengeance and divine justice that broods over
them like a cloud. These memories, still so com-
pelling, have become a part of the old story, inseparable from it. One might almost say, they *are*
the story. In the mood of awe with which we
first pored over the pages of the Doré Bible—if
we can but re-live it for an instant!—Delilah is
no longer a figure familiar to us, a human being
like ourselves. She is Delilah herself, straight out
of the pages of the Old Testament, the "Fury
with the abhorréd shears."

Now the dramatic imagination invests our costume with wonder and awe and a kind of dark glory. It is a costume for Delilah. She—Delilah the enchantress—is to wear it in her moment of triumph over the husband whom she has betrayed and blinded. Another light is thrown upon it, the light of childhood recollection. Images of Circe and Hecate and "dark-veiled Cotytto" come thronging into our minds, with their philters and their potions and their magic spells.

Our exercise draws toward an end. Now, finally, let us see what Milton himself tells us. He compares the figure of Delilah to a ship. A stately ship of Tarsus. Not an English ship, you will note, but Oriental, such a ship, perhaps, as the one that brought Shakespeare's Viola to the stormy coast of Illyria. *And what should I do in Illyria? My brother, he is in Elysium.* . . . The ship of Milton's dreams, sailing on, sailing on, toward the islands of myrrh and cinnamon—! This is not the only time we have seen a woman compared to a ship in dramatic literature. The comparison is a happy one always. The image holds us, whether it is the image of this stately galleon moving slowly athwart our fancy or of the brisk little pleasure-boat, Mistress Millamant,

sweeping in with all sails set and a shoal of fools
for tenders. Or of the tight vessel, Mistress Frail,
well-rigged an she were but as well manned.
There is something feminine, as every man
knows, about all sailing-ships, with their bend-
ings and glidings and swayings. How they set
sail for an occasion and float and veer and turn
and take the air and bow and hesitate and advance
and dissemble! Beautiful ships, beloved of mari-
ners, beautiful women, who charm our hearts
away. . . .

A costume of the Reformation: a Miltonic costume: a gleaming costume: a Biblical costume: a
costume for Delilah: and, finally, a costume that
reminds us of a stately ship. A strange mingling
of images. . . . All at once we see it. The figure
—I had almost said figurehead—draws near and
in our imagination we watch its majestic progress
across the stage. It towers above us on its high
chopines. There is a gleam and a moving of rich
stuffs and shapes and above all a countenance—is
it a mask?—topped by a high jeweled headdress
and bent down ever and again to catch the lights
from below. We have a sense of a thing all
golden, a gilded galleon riding the waves. Golden,

carved, overlaid, crusted with gold on dark gold, so heavy it can move only with a gliding step, a slow, measured approach. The billowing folds of the stiff brocaded Oriental silks make a whispering sound like the sound of waves breaking on the shore. There is a rippling of light and a soft rustling and a foam of lace on the purfled sleeves and a sheen of gems over all, a mirage of sapphires and moonstones and aquamarines and drops of crystal. Great triple ruffs float upon the air, and veils—"slow-dropping veils of thinnest lawn"— droop and fall with the figure's stately dippings and fillings and careenings over the smooth floor of the sea. We see it for an instant, plain and clear.

Now it has vanished.

We saw it. And now we must make it.

VI

LIGHT AND SHADOW IN THE THEATRE

VI

LIGHT AND SHADOW IN THE THEATRE

Put out the light and then—put out the light!
—SHAKESPEARE

*The artist . . . will give us the gloom of gloom
and the sunshine of sunshine.*
—EMERSON

PROFESSOR MAX REINHARDT once said, "I am
told, that the art of lighting a stage consists of
putting light where you want it and taking it
away where you don't want it." I have often had
occasion to think of this remark—so often, in
fact, that with the passage of time it has taken
on for me something of the quality of an old
proverb. Put light where you want it and take it
away where you don't want it. What could be
more simple?

But our real problem in the theatre is to know
where to put the light and where to take it away.
And this, as Professor Reinhardt very well knows,

is not so simple. On the contrary, it demands the knowledge and the application of a lifetime.

Future historians will speak of this period in theatrical history as the spotlight era. Spotlights have become a part of the language of the theatre. Indeed, it is hardly too much to say that they have created our contemporary theatre idiom. Once upon a time our stages were lighted by gas-jets and before that by kerosene lamps, and before that by tapers and torches. And in the days to come we may see some kind of ultra-violet radiation in our theatres, some new fluorescence. But today our productions are characterized—conditioned, one might almost say—by conical shafts of colored electric light which beat down upon them from lamps placed in the flies and along the balconies of the theatre. Lighting a play today is a matter of arranging and rearranging these lamps in an infinite variety of combinations. This is an exercise involving great technical skill and ingenuity. The craft of lighting has been developed to a high degree and it is kept to a high standard by rigorous training in schools and colleges. It has become both exacting and incredibly exact. The beam of light strikes with the precision of a *mot juste.* It bites like an etcher's needle or cuts deep like a surgeon's scalpel. Every tendency moves strongly toward creating an efficient engine behind the proscenium arch. Almost without our knowing it this wonderful invention has become a part of the general *expertise* of Broadway show-business. We handle our spotlights and gelatines and dimmers in the theatre with the same delight and the same sense of mastery with which we drive a high-powered automobile or pilot an aeroplane.

But at rare moments, in the long quiet hours of light-rehearsals, a strange thing happens. We are overcome by a realization of the *livingness* of light. As we gradually bring a scene out of the shadows, sending long rays slanting across a column, touching an outline with color, animating the scene moment by moment until it seems to breathe, our work becomes an incantation. We feel the presence of elemental energies.

There is hardly a stage designer who has not experienced at one time or another this overwhelming sense of the livingness of light. I hold these moments to be among the most precious of all experiences the theatre can give us. The true life of the theatre is in them. At such moments our eyes are opened. We catch disturbing glimpses of a theatre not yet created. Our imaginations leap forward.

It is the memory of these rare moments that inspires us and guides us in our work. While we are studying to perfect ourselves in the use of the intricate mechanism of stage lighting we are learning to transcend it. Slowly, slowly, we begin to see lighting in the theatre, not only as an exciting craft but as an art, at once visionary and exact, subtle, powerful, infinitely difficult to learn. We begin to see that a drama is not an engine, running at full speed from the overture to the final curtain, but a living organism. And we see light as a part of that livingness.

Our first duty in the theatre is always to the actors. It is they who interpret the drama. The stage belongs to them and they must dominate it. Surprising as it may seem, actors are sometimes most effective when they are not seen at all. Do you remember the impact of Orson Welles' broadcast of a threatened Martian invasion? A voice out of darkness. . . . But this, of course, is an exception. In nine cases out of ten our problem is simply that of making the actors and their environment clearly and fully visible.

Visible, yes. But in a very special way. The life we see on the stage is not the everyday life we know. It is—how shall I express it?—*more so.* The world of the theatre is a world of sharper, clearer, swifter impressions than the world we live in. That is why we go to the theatre, to dwell for an hour in this unusual world and draw new life from it. The actors who reveal the heightened life of the theatre should move in a light that is altogether uncommon. It is not enough for us to make them beautiful, charming, splendid. Our purpose must be to give by means of light an impression of something out of the ordinary, away from the mediocre, to make the performance exist in an ideal world of wisdom and understanding. Emerson speaks of a divine aura that breathes through forms. The true actor-light—the true performance-light—is a radiance, a nimbus, a subtle elixir, wherein the characters of the drama may manifest themselves to their audience in their inmost reality.

Perhaps the word *lucid* best describes this light. A lucid light. I think of the exquisite clarity in the prints of Hiroshige. A light of "god-like intellection" pervades these scenes. They are held in a shadowless tranquillity that cannot change. The peace of the first snowfall is in them. Everything is perceived here; everything is understood; everything is known.

Or I might use the word *penetrating*. If we look at a portrait by one of our fashionable portrait-painters and then at a portrait by Rembrandt, we see that the one is concerned mainly with the recording of immediate surface impressions. His approach is that of a journalist who assembles a number of interesting and arresting facts for his leading article. The other penetrates beneath the surface into the inner life of his subject. In the portrait by Rembrandt we see not only the features but the character of the sitter; not only the character, but the soul. We see a life that is not of this moment but of all moments. We sense "the ultimate in the immediate." The portrait of an old man becomes a portrait of old age.

Or I might use the word *aware*. When we see a good play well performed we are brought to the quivering raw edge of experience. We are caught up into the very quick of living. Our senses are dilated and intent. We become preternaturally

aware of each instant of time as it passes. In this
awareness we see the actors more clearly, more
simply, than we have ever seen human beings
before. They seem, in some strange way, more
unified. We no longer appraise them or criticize
them or form opinions about them. We forget all
that we have ever heard or read about them. We
gaze at them as we gaze at long-lost loved ones or
at those we look upon for the last time. *Forever
and forever, farewell, Cassius. . . .* And we see
them in a different light. It is this *different* light
that should be given in the theatre.

But more than all these necessary qualities, the
lighting of a play should contain an element of
surprise, a sense of discovery. It holds the promise of a new and unforgettable experience. I will
give you an illustration. We are all familiar with
the lines from Keats' sonnet, *On First Looking
into Chapman's Homer*—

> *Or like stout Cortez, when with eagle eyes*
> *He stared at the Pacific—and all his men*
> *Looked at each other with a wild surmise*—

Let us put out of our minds for a moment the
accustomed music of these lines and allow the
poet to take us with him on his high adventure.

Imagine this little band of explorers, lost in wonder, on the shore of an unknown ocean. See their faces as the vision of a new world bursts upon them. A scene on the stage should give us the same sense of incredulity and wonder and delight. As we enter the theatre we too are on the threshold of a new experience. The curtain rises. The vision of a new world bursts upon us as it burst upon these voyagers of an earlier day. A new powerful life pervades the theatre. Our hearts beat with a wild hope. Is this what we have waited for? we ask. Shall we see at last? Shall we know?

Lighting a scene consists not only in throwing light upon objects but in throwing light upon a subject. We have our choice of lighting a drama from the outside, as a spectator, or from the inside, as a part of the drama's experience. The objects to be lighted are the forms which go to make up the physical body of the drama—the actors, the setting, the furnishings and so forth. But the subject which is to be lighted is the drama itself. We light the actors and the setting, it is true, but we illuminate the drama. We reveal the drama. We use light as we use words, to elucidate ideas and emotions. Light becomes a tool, an instrument of expression, like a paint-brush, or a sculptor's chisel, or a phrase of music. We turn inward and at once we are in the company of the great ones of the theatre. We learn from them to bathe our productions in the light that never was on sea or land.

One afternoon many years ago I was taken into the inner room of a little picture gallery and there I saw, hanging on the wall opposite me, Albert Pinkham Ryder's painting of *Macbeth and the Witches*. I knew then in a sudden flash of perception that the light that never was on sea or land was a reality and not an empty phrase. My life changed from that moment. Since then I try with all the energy of which I am capable to bring this other light into the theatre. For I know it is the light of the masters.

I find this light of other days in the paintings of Ryder and Redon and Utrillo, in the etchings of Gordon Craig, in Adolphe Appia's drawing of the Elysian Fields from the third act of the *Orpheus* of Gluck. Here it is for everyone to see, achieved once and for all, so clearly stated that no one can escape it. I find it implicit in certain scenes from Shakespeare. It casts its spell upon the lovers, Miranda and Ferdinand, as they meet for the first time on Prospero's magic island. Miranda speaks—

> *What, is't a spirit?*
> *Lord, how it looks about: Believe me, sir,*
> *It carries a brave form. But 'tis a spirit . . .*
> *I might call him*
> *A thing divine, for nothing natural*
> *I ever saw so noble. . . .*

And Ferdinand—

Most sure the goddess
On whom these airs attend . . . my prime request,
Which I do first pronounce, is, O you wonder,
If you be maid or no? . . .

And again, when Prospero by his art calls down the very gods and goddesses from Olympus to celebrate their marriage, Ceres, and great Juno, and Iris with her rainbow—

> *—and thy broom-groves,*
> *Whose shadows the dismissèd bachelor loves,*
> *Being lass-lorn: thy pole-clipt vineyard,*
> *And thy sea-marge, sterile and rocky-hard,*

*Where thou thyself dost air, the Queen o' the
   sky,*
Whose watery arch and messenger am I. . . .

A rare light of the imagination is poured over the
scene, fresh and disturbing and strangely tender.
A new theatre draws near, bathed in "the nameless glow that colors mental vision."

Lucidity, penetration, awareness, discovery, in-
wardness, wonder. . . . These are the qualities
we should try to achieve in our lighting. And
there are other qualities too. There is a quality of
luster, a shine and a gleam that befits the exceptional occasion. (It would be hard perhaps to
make the water-front saloon setting of *Anna
Christie* lustrous, but I am not so sure. It is the
occasion and not the setting which should be lustrous.) There is a quality which I can only describe as racy, a hidalgo quality, proud, self-con-
tained. And last of all, there is a quality of secu-
rity, a bold firm stroke, an authority that puts an
audience at its ease, an assurance that nothing in
the performance could ever go wrong, a strength,
a serenity, flowing down from some inexhaustible
shining spring. Here, in a little circle of clear

radiance, the life of the theatre is going on, a life we can see, and know, and learn to love.

But creating an ideal, exalted atmosphere, an "intenser day" in the theatre is only a part of our task, so small a part that at times it seems hardly to matter at all. However, beautiful or expressive this light may be, it is still not a dramatic light. Rather, it is a lyric light, more suited to feeling than to action. There is no conflict in it: there is only radiance. Great drama is given to us in terms of action, and in illuminating dramatic action we must concern ourselves not only with light, but with shadow.

How shall I convey to you the meaning of shadow in the theatre—the primitive dread, the sense of brooding, of waiting, of fatality, the shrinking, the blackness, the descent into endless night? *The valley of the Shadow. . . . Ye who read are still among the living, but I who write shall have long since gone my way into the region of shadows. . . . Finish, bright lady, the long day is done, and we are for the dark. . . .* It is morning, the sun shines, the dew is on the grass, and God's in His Heaven. We have just risen from sleep. We are young, the sap runs strong in us, and we stretch ourselves and laugh. Then the sun rises higher, and it is high noon, and the light is clear, and colors are bright, and life shines out in a splendid fullness. Jack has his Jill, and Benedick his Beatrice, and Millamant her Mirabell. But then the sun sinks down, the day draws to its close, the shadows gather, and darkness comes, and voices fall lower, and we hear the whisper, and the stealthy footfall, and we see the light in the cranny of the door, and the low star reflected in the stagnant tarn. A nameless fear descends upon us. Ancient apparitions stir in the shadows. We listen spellbound to the messengers from another world, the unnatural horrors that visit us in the night.

I shall leave the doctors of psychology to explain the connection between this ancient terror and the dread of the unknown darkness in our minds which they have begun to call the subconscious. It is enough for us to know that the connection exists, and that it is the cause of the curious hold which light and shadow can exercise over the imagination of an audience. At heart we are all children afraid of the dark, and our fear goes back to remote beginnings of the human race. See the mood of an audience change, hear them chatter or fall silent, as the lights in the theatre are raised or lowered. See them rush to the nearest exit at the sudden rumor, "The lights have gone out!" See their instant reassurance as the broken circuit is repaired and the great chandelier blazes once more. It is such instinctive responses that give light its dynamic power in the theatre.

Our greatest dramatists have woven light and shadow into their creations. Dramatic literature is filled with examples. We see Lavinia Mannon as she closes the shutters of the Mannon house, banishing herself forever from the light of day. We see the moon shining fitfully through scudding storm-clouds over the ramparts of Elsinore, where the unquiet ghost of Hamlet's father wanders, wrapped in his black cloak, "for to go invisibell." We hear the tortured cry of Claudius, "Give me some light! Away!" The dim shadows of Pelléas and Mélisande embrace one another far away at the end of the garden;—*Comme nos ombres sont grandes ce soir! . . . Oh! quelles s'embrassent loin de nous!* . . . We watch the two women in the anteroom of Lucio Settala's studio as they gaze at one another across the shaft of light that falls along the floor between them. We wander with Lear through a storm that is like a convulsion of Nature, "a tyranny of the open night," an "extremity of the skies."

Here is the most wonderful example of all, the great classic example of dramatic insight:

Lo, you, here she comes! This is her very guise,
and, upon my life, fast asleep. Observe her:
stand close.
How came she by that light?
Why, it stood by her. She has light by her con-
tinually, 'Tis her command.
You see, her eyes are open.
Ay, but their sense is shut.
What is it she does now?

Shakespeare animates the scene with his own intense mood. The candle flame lives in the theatre. It becomes a symbol of Lady Macbeth's own life —flickering, burning low, vanishing down into darkness. *Out, Out, brief candle!* . . . Where the layman might see nothing more than an actual candle, made of wax, bought for so much, at such and such a place, the dramatist has seen a great revealing image. He has seen deep into the meaning of this terrible moment, and the taper is a part of it. *Animula, vagula, blandula,* little flame, little breath, little soul, moving before us for the last time. . . . And the shadow on the wall behind "that broken lady" becomes an omen, a portent, a presage of her "sad and solemn slumbers," a dark companion following her, silent and implacable, as she passes from this to that other world. *She should have died hereafter. Life's but a walking shadow.* . . . When we think of this scene we remember, not only the dreadful words and the distraught figure, all in white like a shroud; we see vast spaces and enveloping darkness and a tiny trembling light and a great malevolent shadow. The icy fear that grips us is built up out of all these elements. And when we put the scene on the stage we do not serve Shakespeare's drama as we should serve it until we have given each of these elements its full value and its proper emphasis.

As we dwell upon these great examples of the use of light in the theatre we cease to think of harmony and beauty and think instead of energy, contrast, violence, struggle, shock. We dream of a light that is tense and vivid and full of temperament, an impulsive, wayward, capricious light, a light "haunted with passion," a light of flame and tempest, a light which draws its inspiration from the moods of light in Nature, from the illimitable night sky, the blue dusk, the halcyon light that broods over the western prairies. We say with D'Annunzio, *I would that Nature could be round my creations as our oldest forefathers saw her: the passionate actress in an immortal drama.* . . . Here before us as we dream is the frame of the proscenium, enclosing a darkness like the darkness that quivers behind our closed eyelids. And now the dark stage begins to burn and glow under our fingers, burning like the embers of the forge of Vulcan, and shafts of light stab through the darkness, and shadows leap and shudder, and we are in the regions where splendor and terror move. We are practicing an art of light and shadow that was old before the Pyramids, an art that can shake our dispositions with thoughts beyond the reaches of our souls.

The creative approach to the problem of stage lighting—the art, in other words, of knowing where to put light on the stage and where to take it away—is not a matter of textbooks or precepts. There are no arbitrary rules. There is only a goal and a promise. We have the mechanism with which to create this ideal, exalted, dramatic light in the theatre. Whether we can do so or not is a matter of temperament as well as of technique. The secret lies in our perception of light in the theatre as something alive.

Does this mean that we are to carry images of poetry and vision and high passion in our minds while we are shouting out orders to electricians on ladders in light-rehearsals?

Yes. This is what it means.

VII

TOWARD A NEW STAGE

VII

TOWARD A NEW STAGE

What is called realism is usually a record of life at a low pitch and ebb viewed in the sunless light of day.

—WALTER DE LA MARE

In our fine arts not imitation but creation is the aim.

—EMERSON

ONCE again the air of Broadway is filled with the gloomy forebodings of the self-styled prophets of the theatre who are busy assuring us for the thousandth time that the theatre is dying. In the past we have not taken these prophecies of doom too seriously, for we have observed that the theatre is always dying and always being reborn, Phoenix-like, at the very moment when we have finished conducting the funeral service over its ashes. But this time there is a greater content of truth in what the prophets are telling us. The theatre we knew, the theatre we grew up in, has recently begun to show unmistakable symptoms of decline. It is dwindling and shrinking away, and presently it will be forgotten.

Let us look at this dying theatre for a moment. It is essentially a prose theatre, and of late it has become increasingly a theatre of journalism. The quality of legend is almost completely absent from contemporary plays. They appear to be uneasily conscious of the camera and the phonograph. There are brilliant exceptions to this generalization—I need mention only *Green Pastures, Strange Interlude,* or Sophie Treadwell's exciting *Saxophone*—but in the main the dramas of our time are as literal as if they had been dictated by the village iceman or by a parlor-maid peering through a keyhole.

It is this theatre that is dying. Motion pictures are draining the very life-blood from its veins.

Disquieting as this may be to the purveyors of show-business, there is a kind of cosmic logic in it. The theatre of our time grew up on a photographic basis and it would have continued to function contentedly on this basis for many years to come if motion pictures had not been invented. But nothing can be so photographic as a photograph, especially when that photograph moves and speaks. Motion pictures naturally attract to themselves everything that is factual, objective, explicit. Audiences are gradually coming to prefer realism on the screen to realism in the theatre. Almost insensibly Hollywood has brought an irresistible pressure to bear upon the realistic theatre and the picture-frame stage. Future generations may find it hard to believe that such things ever existed.

These statements are not to be construed as an adverse criticism of motion pictures. On the contrary: motion pictures have begun to take on a new life of their own, a life of pure thought, and they are becoming more alive every day. The fact is that in our time the theatre has become mixed, confused, a hybrid. A play can be made from almost any novel and a motion picture can be made from almost any play. What this means is that the theatre has not yet been brought to its own perfection. Literature is literature and theatre is theatre and motion pictures are motion pictures, but the theatre we know is all these things mixed together and scrambled. But now—fortunately, some of us believe—we may note an increasing tendency toward the separation of these various arts, each into its own characteristic form. Motion pictures are about to become a great liberating agent of drama. By draining the theatre of its literalness they are giving it back to imagination again.

Think of it! No more copybook dialogue, no more drug-store clerks drafted to impersonate themselves in real drug-stores transferred bodily to the stage, no more unsuccessful attempts to prove to us that we are riding the waves of the Atlantic Ocean with Columbus instead of sitting in a theatre, no more tasteful, well-furnished rooms with one wall missing. . . . A theatre set free for beauty and splendor and dreams—

Of late years realism in the theatre has become more and more closely bound up with the idea of the "stage picture." But now it would seem that this idea is about to be done away with once and for all. The current conception of stage scenery as a more or less accurate representation of an actual scene—organized and simplified, to be sure, but still essentially a representation—is giving way to another conception of something far less actual and tangible. It is a truism of theatrical history that stage pictures become important only in periods of low dramatic vitality. Great dramas do not need to be illustrated or explained or embroidered. They need only to be brought to life on the stage. The reason we have had realistic stage "sets" for so long is that few of the dramas of our time have been vital enough to be able to dispense with them. That is the plain truth. Actually the best thing that could happen to our theatre at this moment would be for playwrights and actors and directors to be handed a bare stage on which no scenery could be placed, and then told that they must write and act and direct for this stage. In no time we should have the most exciting theatre in the world.

The task of the stage designer is to search for all sorts of new and direct and unhackneyed ways whereby he may establish the *sense of place.* The purpose of a stage setting, whatever its form, whether it be for tragedy, comedy, history, pastoral, pastoral-comical, historical-pastoral, tragical-historical, tragical-comical-historical-pastoral, scene individable or poem unlimited, is simply this: *to remind the audience of where the actors are supposed to be.* A true stage-setting is an invocation to the *genius loci*—a gesture "enforcing us to this place"—and nothing more. The theatre we know occupies itself with creating stage "illusion." What we are now interested in, however, is not illusion, but allusion, and allusion to the most magical beauty. *I seek less,* said Walt Whitman, *to display any theme or thought and more to bring you into the atmosphere of the theme or thought—there to pursue your own flight.* This is precisely the aim of stage designing, to bring the audience into the atmosphere of the theme or thought. Any device will be acceptable so long as it succeeds in carrying the audience along with it.

The loveliest and most poignant of all stage pictures are those that are seen in the mind's eye. All the elaborate mechanism of our modern stage cannot match for real evocation the line, *Tom's a-cold.* A mere indication of place can send our imaginations leaping. *We'll 'een to't like French falcons, fly at anything we see.* . . . It is this delighted exercise of imagination, this heady joy, that the theatre has lost and is about to find once more. Call upon this faculty—so strangely latent in all of us—and it responds at once, swift as Ariel to the summons of Prospero.

Shakespeare could set his stage with a phrase.
Listen—

> *This castle hath a pleasant seat; the air*
> *Nimbly and sweetly recommends itself*
> *Unto our gentle senses. . . .*

Listen again—

> *Now we bear the king*
> *Toward Calais; grant him there; there seen,*
> *Heave him away upon your wingèd thoughts*
> *Athwart the sea. . . .*

And here is William Butler Yeats' introduction
to *The Only Jealousy of Emer*—

> *I call before the eyes a roof*
> *With cross-beams darkened by smoke.*
> *A fisher's net hangs from a beam,*
> *A long oar lies against the wall.*
> *I call up a poor fisher's house. . . .*

And here is the speech of Hakuryo the Fisher-
man in the Japanese No drama, *Hagoromo,* so
beautifully translated by Fenollosa—

> *I am come to shore. I disembark at Matsubara.*
> *It is just as they told me. A cloudless sky, a rain*

of flowers, strange fragrance all about me. These are no common things. Nor is this cloak that hangs upon the pine tree.

And finally—to take a more familiar example—here is a passage from Thornton Wilder's play, *Our Town*. The narrator is speaking—

This is our doctor's house—Doc Gibbs'. This is the back door.

Two arched trellises are pushed out, one by each proscenium pillar.

There's some scenery for those who think they have to have scenery.

There's a garden here. Corn . . . peas . . . beans . . . hollyhocks. . . .

These stage directions (for that is what they are; they direct us) evoke the *locale* and the mood of the particular drama in question with great ease and with great economy of means. How simple they are, and how telling, and how right! A few words, and the life-giving dramatic imagination answering the summons, fresh, innocent, immensely powerful, eagerly obedient.

In Shakespeare's day the written and the spoken word held a peculiar magic, as of something new-born. With this exciting new medium of dramatic expression at hand it was simple for a playwright to transport his audience from place to place by a spoken stage-direction,

In fair Verona, where we lay our scene . . .

or by a legend, THIS IS MASTER JONAH JACK-DAWE'S HOUSE, or, PLAIN NEAR SALISBURY, painted on a signboard. A printed legend seen on our stage today would arouse only a momentary curiosity, or at most a pleasure akin to that of examining some antique stage trapping in a museum, a sword once handled by Burbage, a letter penned by Bernhardt. There is little to be gained by attempting to re-establish such purely literary indications of place in the theatre. But the spoken word still retains its power to enchant and transport an audience, and this power has recently been enhanced to an extraordinary and altogether unpredictable degree by the inventions of the sound amplifier and the radio transmitter. The technicians of the radio learned long ago to induce the necessary sense of place by means of spoken descriptions and so-called "sound-effects." These devices have caught the imagination of radio audiences. They are accepted without question and cause no surprise. We can hardly imagine a radio drama without them. It is odd that our playwrights and stage designers have not yet sensed the limitless potentialities of this new enhancement of the spoken word. A magical new medium of scenic evocation is waiting to be pressed into service. Imagine a Voice pervading a theatre from all directions at once, enveloping us, enfolding us, whispering to us of scenes "beautiful as pictures no man drew" . . .

Today we are more picture-minded than word-minded. But what we hear in the theatre must again take its place beside what we see in the theatre. If we are to enhance the spoken word by any means whatever we must first be sure that it is worth enhancing. Here is a direct challenge to our dramatists and our actors to clothe ideas in expressive speech and to give words once again their high original magic.

Imaginative minds have been at work in our theatre for years and they stand ready to create new scenic conventions at a moment's notice. We may look with profit at a few of the outstanding productions of these years. *The Cradle Will Rock:* A neutral-tinted cyclorama. A double row

of chairs in which the members of the cast are
seated in full view of the audience. An upright
piano set slantwise near the footlights. The author enters, sits at the piano, plays a few bars of
music, announces the various members of the
cast, who bow in turn as their names are men-
tioned. Then he says simply, The first scene is
laid in a night court. Two actors rise and speak
the first lines. The play has begun. . . . *Julius
Caesar:* The bare brick walls of the stage of the
Mercury Theatre stained blood-red from floor to
gridiron. The lighting equipment fully visible. A
wide low platform set squarely in the center of
the stage. A masterly handling of the crowds and
some superb acting. . . . Stravinsky's *Oedipus
Rex* presented by the League of Composers: The
great stage of the Metropolitan Opera House a
deep blue void out of which emerge the towering
marionettes who symbolize the protagonists of
the drama. Their speeches declaimed in song
by blue-robed soloists and a blue-robed chorus
grouped in a pyramid on the stage below them.
. . . The procession of wet black umbrellas in
the funeral scene of *Our Town.* The little toy
Ark in *Green Pastures.* The Burning Bush in the
same play, a tiny faded Christmas tree with a few

colored electric light bulbs hanging on it. Best of all, and ever to be remembered, the March of the Pilgrims to the Promised Land on a treadmill retrieved from a musical comedy and put by the author to an exalted use of which its original inventor had never dreamed. And there are many others.

Audiences have found these productions thoroughly convincing. Their delighted acceptance of the imaginative conventions employed gives proof —if proof be needed—that the unrealistic idea has come into the theatre to stay. Whether the particular devices I have noted are to be adopted in future or not is a matter of no importance. We may take courage from them to move forward boldly and with confidence.

Newer and more imaginative scenic conventions will presently become firmly established in the theatre and representations of place will be superseded by evocations of the sense of place. Then the stage designer can turn his attention away from the problem of creating stage settings to the larger and far more engrossing problem of creating stages. For the primary concern of the stage designer is with stages, and not with stage settings. All our new devices for scenic evocation will be ineffective except in an exciting environment. The new drama and its new stage setting will require a new type of stage. What will this new stage be like?

First of all it will be presented frankly for what it is, a stage. I have never been able to understand why the stages of our theatres should invariably be so ugly. Theatre owners take great pains to make the auditoriums of their theatres glowing and cheerful and comfortable, but what we call a stage today is nothing more than a bare brick box fretted with radiator pipes. Why should this be so? One would think that a stage was something to be ashamed of, to be hidden away like an idiot child. Surely the first step toward creating a new stage is to make it an exciting thing in itself.

This stage will be simple, with the simplicity of the stages of the great theatres of the past. We shall turn again to the traditional, ancient stage, the platform, the *tréteau,* the boards that actors have trod from time out of mind. What we need in the theatre is a space for actors to act in, a space reserved for them where they may practice their immemorial art of holding the mirror up to na-

ture. They will be able to move with ease to and
from this space, they will be able to make their
appropriate exits and entrances. We shall find a
way to bathe these actors in expressive and dramatic light. And that is all.

I am looking forward to a theatre, a stage, a
production, that will be exciting to the point of
astonishment. Behind the proscenium will stand
a structure of great beauty, existing in dignity, a
Precinct set apart. It will be distinguished, aus-
tere, sparing in detail, rich in suggestion. It will
carry with it a high mood of awe and eagerness.
Like the great stages of the past, it will be an integral part of the structure of the theatre itself,
fully visible at all times. Will this stage be too
static, too inflexible, too "harshly frugal" for audiences to accept? Not at all. If it is beautiful and
exciting and expressive we shall not tire of it.
Moreover, its mood will be continually varied by
changes of light.

Our new-old stage—this architectural structure
sent through moods by light—will serve as never
before to rivet our attention upon the actors' performance. It will remind us all over again that
great drama is always presented to us in terms of
action. In the ever-shifting tableaux of Shake-

speare's plays, in the flow of the various scenes, he gives us an incessant visual excitement. Once we have arrived at an understanding of the inner pattern of any one of his plays and can externalize it on Shakespeare's own stage we discover an unsuspected visual brilliance arising directly from the variety of the action. It is the performance, not the setting, which charms us. The fixed stage becomes animated through the movement of the actors. All good actors will respond like thoroughbred race-horses to the challenge.

This fixed, impersonal, dynamic environment will be related to the particular drama in question by slight and subtle indications of place and mood—by ingenious arrangements of the necessary properties, by the groupings of the actors, by an evocative use of sound and light. Then the actors will be left free to proceed with the business of performance. In this connection we may again note a striking characteristic of radio drama. A stage setting remains on the stage throughout the action of any particular scene. But the setting of a radio drama is indicated at the beginning of the performance and then quietly dismissed. Radio audiences do not find it necessary to remain conscious of the setting during the action of the drama. They become absorbed in the performance at once. Why should not this be true of theatre audiences as well? Here is an idea that is filled with far-reaching suggestion for our stage designers. Can it be that the stage settings of today are too much with us, late and soon? Would not a setting be more effective if it were merely an indication of the atmosphere of the play offered to the audience for a moment at the beginning of the performance and then taken away again?

If we discard for a moment the idea of a setting as something that must act all through a play along with the actors and think of it instead as a brief ceremony of welcome, so to speak, a toast to introduce the speakers of the evening, all sorts of arresting and exciting visual compositions occur to us. Scenery takes wings, becomes once more a part of the eternal flight and fantasy of the theatre. Let us imagine a few of these "transitory shows of things." A curtain lifted at the back of the stage to reveal a momentary glimpse of a giant painting of the park on Sorin's estate—the First Act of *The Sea Gull*. A delicate arrangement of screens and ironwork laced with moonlight for the setting of a modern drawing-room comedy, visible at the rise of the curtain, then gliding imperceptibly out of sight. A motion-picture screen lowered at the beginning of the performance of *He Who Gets Slapped*, the life of the little circus given to the audience in a series of screen "wipe-outs." A group of actors arranged in a vividly expressive tableau at the rise of the curtain to evoke a battle-scene from *Richard III*, dissolving into the action of the play. And so on. Such ideas may seem far-fetched, but they are by no means so far-fetched as we might be inclined to believe.

No one seriously interested in the theatre can be anything but overjoyed at the encroachments of Hollywood upon Broadway. Hollywood is doing what the artists of our theatre have been trying to do for years. It is drawing realism out of the theatre as the legendary madstone—the Bezoar of the ancients—drew the madness from a lunatic patient. The only theatre worth saving, the only theatre worth having, is a theatre motion pictures cannot touch. When we succeed in eliminating from it every trace of the photographic attitude of mind, when we succeed in making a production that is the exact antithesis of a motion picture, a production that is everything a motion picture is not and nothing a motion picture is, the old lost magic will return once more. The realistic theatre, we may remember, is less than a hundred years old. But the theatre— great theatre. world theatre—is far older than that, so many centuries older that by comparison it makes our little candid-camera theatre seem like something that was thought up only the day before yesterday. We need not be impatient. A brilliant fresh theatre will presently appear.

VIII

BEHIND THE SCENES

VIII

BEHIND THE SCENES

And now the play is played out, and of rhetoric enough.

—SOCRATES

And is life not like the play? The gods who watch the drama know that somebody must play the villain's part, and somebody the pauper's. . . . He, therefore, who is wise plays pauper, king, or villain with the gods in mind.

—TALBOT MUNDY

THE TAXI drops me at the old Nixon Theatre in Pittsburgh. I have traveled all day to come here. It is late. I go up the dark dirty alley littered with newspapers and refuse, to the grimy old sign, STAGE DOOR. Inside, the doorman, the letter-rack, the dark stage with its one tiny pilot-lamp, a pin-point of light in a region of shadows. The stage is lonely, and forlorn, and as silent as midnight. Ropes descend from the darkness of the flies, dim curtains fade away into mystery. How well I know these stages, with their chill, brooding at-

151

mosphere, their echoes and their memories! Here, in this Cimmerian darkness, in this strange sunless Acheron, dwell the great spirits of the Theatre. I feel them in the air around me.

A partly assembled setting is standing on the stage. I see the walls of a room hung with pictures and elaborate window-draperies. I walk around the setting and go behind it. There is no back. Only a wooden framework covered with canvas, stamped with the name of the scene-painter and blackened by the handling of numberless stage-hands. Behind this scene, which will presently seem so real when viewed from the front, there is nothing. Nothing at all. Only the empty echoing stage, desolate, ominous, prophetic.

I stand for a while in the shadowy wings, in the half-light that brings dreams. Here, I say to myself, is where actors spend their lives. It is their only home. A strange home for anyone to have, this comfortless chill void.

I go into the old green-room. I look at the faded photographs of bygone celebrities, the sons and daughters of Thespis, yellowed and blurred. The mask of Lear's fool seems laid over these faces, with their mobile features, their large eyes, their sensitive mouths, their sad wise air of the seasoned player—over-emphatic brave faces of those who have dared to pass out of life into the life of the theatre. There is a certain pathos about these figures. I think of the Saturday night parties, the jumps on trains, the bustling up alleys in the dark, the knowledge of a life backstage, behind the scenes. . . .

Why did these actors go into the theatre? Why did they choose to paint their faces, learn endless lines, get up on the stage before audiences? Perhaps they themselves did not know. They were drawn to the theatre by some nameless ambition to dominate, it may be, some desire to "show off," or by some half-grasped intuition as to the nature of their chosen calling. But no matter how they began, they presently became part of the Body of the Theatre, as people become part of the Body of the Church. They became the Ladies and Gentlemen of the Theatre.

Not all of them were born in the theatre, but all of them were born for the theatre, born to tread the boards, to wear the sock and buskin. They sensed the theatre with a kind of sixth sense. In due time they came to look at life in a way that was peculiarly theatrical. They came to see all life in terms of impersonation.

We speak of a scientific attitude toward life, or of a philosophical attitude, or of a religious attitude. But of all conceivable attitudes the theatrical attitude is the most truly creative. To see life as these actors saw it is to move in a realm of truth inhabited by few. Our poets and visionaries attain to this truth in rare and isolated moments of detachment. But audiences come face to face with it every night of their lives—yes, and twice a day on Wednesdays and Saturdays—in every theatre, at every performance. It lies at the root of all dramatic instinct, and it is the essence of the art of acting.

It happens to each one of us at times to feel separated from ourselves, going through the business of living as if we were at once a character in a play and the actor who impersonates that character. Two people dwell in us, an outer self, a being who answers to the name of John Doe or Richard Roe, a kind of character-part, so to speak, and an inner self, a mysterious essence, a hidden flame, a shy wild Harlequin who plays this part before the world. We feel the presence of this other self when some moment of stark reality strikes through the conventions of our everyday lives. There is no one who has not experienced at some time or other the sense of inward withdrawal. All life is indeed a play in which we act out our roles until the final curtain falls. This idea of the theatre goes deep. We recognize its truth in our inmost hearts. We know that it is true as we know that our souls are immortal. I am persuaded that the consciousness of a dual personality—the sense of otherness, of apartness, the sense that we are possessed, that another's voice ever and again speaks through us—is a thing that is very common in human experience and that it is the only thing that separates us from the brutes. Perhaps it was the sense of *theatre* that made us human, ages ago.

If it is true—as Shakespeare makes the melancholy Jaques say—that all the world's a stage, and all the men and women merely players, playing our many parts on "a vaster place than any stage," it follows that we must be playing these parts before an audience. Who and what is that audience? Shall we ever know? Perhaps it is an unseen audience, a hierarchy of invisible powers, the Great Republic of "etherial dominations" that Blake and Shelley saw. I think of the unseen audiences of Toscanini, made free of his art by the miracle of radio transmission. . . . Or is the earth itself a living, sentient being, as the poets have told us, and is it her approval for which we strive, all unknowing, in our performances? And when the curtain has fallen on the last act of our lives, if we have played our parts to the best of our ability, may we hope to hear from beyond the curtain some vibration of divine reassurance, some echo as of ghostly applause?

And is there an Author of the piece, who assigns to each of us his part and makes us "masters of all this world"? And shall we one day be allotted other parts to be acted on other and yet vaster stages? Or shall we return again and again until all parts are played and drama itself is finished?

These players became aware of the profound duality of life at the moment when they spoke their first lines on a stage, and thereafter all their acting was animated by it. They called it giving a good performance. But what they meant was that a spirit was present in them for a time, making them say things that they themselves did not know they knew. This knowledge took its toll of them. They paid for it with a part of their souls. No wonder theirs was a Profession set apart.

The thing that is absent from these records is the thing that never can be recorded, the emotion that these artists aroused in our hearts, the sense of triumph they gave us. Their peculiar power lay in this, that in their impersonations they could show us man's creating spirit, in action, before our eyes. They did not teach or preach about life or explain it or expound it or illustrate it. They created it—life itself, at its fullest and truest and highest.

And in the end they put aside the make-up and the vesture and went away into the darkness, leaving us only a few fading photographs and old playbills, and their imperishable memories.

Alone with their secret, in the old green-room, I think of the words of Plotinus: *For the soul, a divine thing, a fragment as it were of the primal Being, makes beautiful according to their capacity all things whatsoever that it grasps and moulds.*